Dartmoor National Park

A celebration of its people, places and wildlife

Dartmoor National Park

A celebration of its people, places and wildlife

To James,
Best wishes,
Andrew Cooper

Andrew Cooper

green books

First published in 2011 by

Green Books
Dartington Space, Dartington Hall,
Totnes, Devon TQ9 6EN

Photographs by Andrew Cooper
Design by Jayne Jones
Map by Jennifer Johnson

ISBN 978 1 900322 83 6

Printed on Regency Satin paper
by Latimer Trend, Plymouth, UK

The views expressed in this publication are not necessarily those of
the Dartmoor National Park Authority.

The Bronze Age arrowhead pictured on page 131 was photographed with kind permission of the Royal Albert Memorial Museum.
The Bellever pottery on the same page was photographed with kind permission of Dartmoor National Park Authority.

Contents

Acknowledgements

This book could not have been written without the knowledge of so many people who willingly gave their time, not just Dartmoor National Park Authority staff but others who live and work on Dartmoor. I would particularly like to thank Dr Kevin Bishop and John Weir for their enthusiasm and expert guidance, and other staff of the Authority for answering my endless queries with such good humour. My appreciation is especially due to those who shared with me their memories of the moor, providing a remarkable insight into the enjoyment and inspiration that Dartmoor offers. And for revealing more arduous and hilarious times too. It was a pleasure and a privilege to talk to you all.

My special thanks must go to Green Books: to John Elford, Amanda Cuthbert, Alethea Doran, Jayne Jones, Stacey Hedge, Susie Hallam, Bee West and Jon Clift for their considerable publishing expertise and endless patience.

Further reading

Dartmoor, L. A. Harvey & D. St Leger-Gordon (1977). Collins New Naturalist series
Dartmoor, Ian Mercer (2009). Collins New Naturalist series

Dartmoor National Park Authority also publishes many useful and informative leaflets, and its website is a valuable Dartmoor resource - see www.dartmoor-npa.gov.uk

To my wife Jeanne, for her constant encouragement and for the fun family days we spent with our children on the moors. And to our granddaughter Elisabeth, that she may continue to enjoy Dartmoor and revel in its wild beauty.

Last, but not least, to all who strive to maintain Dartmoor's special qualities.

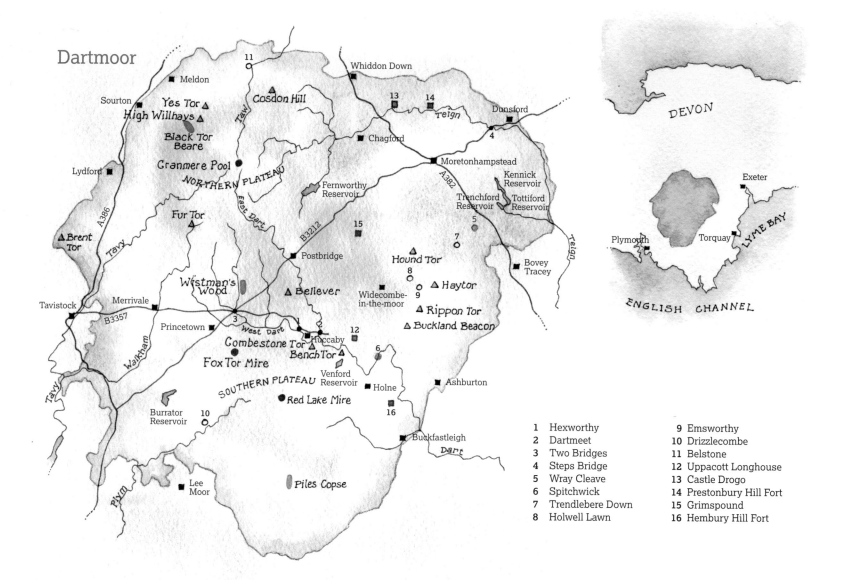

Dartmoor

Meldon
Sourton
Yes Tor △
High Willhays △
Black Tor Beare
Cranmere Pool
NORTHERN PLATEAU
Lydford
Fur Tor △
△ Brent Tor
Tavistock
Merrivale
B3357
Princetown
West Dart
Combestone Tor △
Bench Tor △
Fox Tor Mire
SOUTHERN PLATEAU
Venford Reservoir
Holne
Red Lake Mire
Burrator Reservoir
Lee Moor
Piles Copse
Plym

11
Cosdon Hill
Taw
East Dart
B3212
Postbridge
Wistman's Wood
△ Bellever
Widecombe-in-the-moor
Huccaby
3
Walkham
Tavy

Whiddon Down
13
14
Dunsford
4
Teign
Chagford
Moretonhampstead
A382
Fernworthy Reservoir
Kennick Reservoir
Trenchford Reservoir
Tottiford Reservoir
15
5
7
Hound Tor
8
9 △ Haytor
△ Rippon Tor
△ Buckland Beacon
12
6
Ashburton
16
Buckfastleigh
Dart
Bovey Tracey
Teign

DEVON
Exeter
Plymouth
Torquay
LYME BAY
ENGLISH CHANNEL

1	Hexworthy	9	Emsworthy
2	Dartmeet	10	Drizzlecombe
3	Two Bridges	11	Belstone
4	Steps Bridge	12	Uppacott Longhouse
5	Wray Cleave	13	Castle Drogo
6	Spitchwick	14	Prestonbury Hill Fort
7	Trendlebere Down	15	Grimspound
8	Holwell Lawn	16	Hembury Hill Fort

Foreword

For over 40 years Dartmoor has been part of our landscape. On a clear morning, when we open our bedroom window, we look out over the Okement valley to Yes Tor. Winter usually begins with a sighting of snow up there on the hills - sometimes just a scattering on the highest points, but just as often a thick white blanket, which stays for days, weeks even, and tells us that winter is really here.

As the seasons change our view changes too. On clear frosty days you can almost see the individual granite rocks, even though they are a good 15 miles away. As spring arrives and the air gets warmer, our view becomes hazy and the hills become more gentle, less menacing. In summer Dartmoor is clear again and so beautiful in the evening light, the hills glow in the sunset. Autumn brings the mists - sometimes our valley is enveloped in a soft duvet and the cows drift legless over the water meadows - until the sun breaks through and we can see the hills, serene as ever, full of magic.

Dartmoor has played a strong part in both our lives. As a child, Clare used to visit the moors with her father and together they followed the streams as they tumbled down through the granite boulders. Later we brought our own children to walk along the Dart, watching for dippers and kingfishers as we went. We went to Wistman's Wood and marvelled at the remains of the ancient oak forest. When we started Farms for City Children in 1976 we wanted to share our love of the moors with the children who came to stay with us, taking them for picnics and hikes across the moor.

When Michael wrote *War Horse* in 1982 we had no idea how the book would be received. The story of Joey the farm horse, bought by the army in the First World War, and Albert, the boy who loved him and who left his village to go and look for him and bring him home, was inspired so much by the people who lived in our village and the lives they had led, all in the shadow of Dartmoor. Now Spielberg's film of the book will bring our beautiful countryside to viewers all over the world. Even if they never come here themselves, we know a little of Dartmoor will find its way into their hearts.

Clare and Michael Morpurgo,
Nethercott House, North Devon, October 2011

Preface
Past, present and future

Standing on one of the great granite outcrops encircling 'the moors', as locals like to call the uplands, whatever the weather you cannot fail to be inspired and humbled by the scenery. Come sun, snow, cloud, wind or rain, your view will be enriched by vast skies, deep valleys and rock-strewn hills. Everywhere the sense of remoteness and isolation is reinforced by the roughness of the terrain and places where wildlife thrives.

Today, 60 years is no longer considered to be a lifetime in Britain, and memories of Dartmoor's own story as a national park that began in 1951 are still fresh in the minds of many people. Yet much water has flowed beneath its granite bridges during the course of its history. For all of us, exploring Dartmoor is a journey through time and countless generations of lives. To be found here are ancient farms huddled against slopes, villages nestled between high hills, rough stone walls enclosing fields and rivers weaving their way around enormous boulders. Bog and mire cover vast areas of sodden moor, and in river valleys dampness pervades the air, moss covers the rocks and trees, ferns sprout from every crevice and birdsong mingles with the rush of water. Time hardly seems to have touched these parts, yet much of modern Dartmoor is very different.

In the early days of the National Park, relatively few people had access to cars and the joy of a family outing to the area was simply to play on the moorland and to wade in its cool, clear streams - not that much has changed from those days. But back then it was not uncommon to see cars struggling up the steepest hills, breakdowns queuing in the passing places with bonnets raised, engines steaming and owners fuming. Every summer the chatter of excited children filled the most attractive and accessible moorland spots as happy families tucked into their picnics. For me, watching salmon spawn or a buzzard ride the breeze, the sense of achievement in conquering a tor, or simply letting the wind tug at my coat, were all some of my earliest and fondest childhood recollections. I am sure Dartmoor helped mould me as much as it has many others.

Dartmoor has become a better place for its National Park status, and its worth as an economic asset is becoming

Wild bluebells at Emsworthy, one of Dartmoor's special places.

increasingly recognised. Britain herself is richer for Dartmoor's wildlife, archaeology, landscape, produce and character. Today, the aspirations and efforts of those who first conceived Britain's national parks are continued on Dartmoor by the people committed to its careful management, evolution, conservation and preservation. Only with the goodwill and hard work of so many individuals and organisations who care so deeply about Dartmoor will these uplands continue to provide a place for us all to enjoy. However, for all its ruggedness, the National Park remains incredibly fragile, and managing its various politics, pressures and tensions will prove little compared with the future impact of climate change. Science tells us that no place remains the same, but we must strive to maintain Dartmoor's special qualities, whatever the natural outcomes and differences of opinion, for the benefit of its own distinctive nature and for our future generations.

Introduction
Dartmoor – a national icon

This is the story of Dartmoor, one of the most famous and popular national parks in Britain. A place that can trace its origins back to the dawn of the age of dinosaurs; a story 280 million years in the making.

In the far south-west of Britain, Dartmoor's rugged, windswept twin plateaux tower high above Devon's lush, farmed hills. Renowned as the largest and last great area of wild landscape in the south of England, it is a world apart from the surrounding, gentler countryside. Two of its peaks, High Willhays and Yes Tor, boast the lofty status of being the only mountains in southern England, but other hills abound. All known simply as tors, the most striking are often crowned by imposing fractured piles of granite. The rest are frequently smoother where the underlying rock is less obvious, hidden beneath thin close-cropped turf.

On these high tops the weather can change in a matter of minutes, and the moor can be unforgiving in its harshness. Dartmoor is bleak during the coldest months of winter and often desolate beyond belief, the silence broken only by the rush of wind or lashing horizontal rain. Flocks of hardy sheep or herds of tough ponies that roam freely often seem to be the only sign of life, but even they vanish when blizzards bring heavy falls of snow drifting high against the tors and straggling stone walls. In these almost sub-Arctic conditions, monstrous icicles grow down granite faces forming frozen cascades, while in the valleys snow-laden branches hang low over streams, now ribbons of ice.

As the days begin to lengthen, the growing strength of the sun starts to melt the ice, and soon the sound of rushing water returns. Swollen by the melting snow and torrential rain, dark peat-laden streams quickly rise full to overflowing, and rivers turn to raging white water. Compared with the rest of lowland Devon, spring comes late up here. Fresh green foliage and the first wild flowers gradually make a welcome return, as if creeping up from the lowlands through the wooded valleys, blanketing slopes in vigorous new growth. The appearance of wild daffodils, bluebells and the unfurling fronds of bracken are accompanied by the bubbling cry of curlew and the heart-warming call of the

Facing page: Clapper bridge at Postbridge over the East Dart, thought to date from the thirteenth century.

Dry stone granite walls are a striking feature of Dartmoor.

mew overhead while passing ravens 'cronk' and skylarks pour their song from a brilliant blue sky. Soon the air is laced with the scent of heather and bees busily forage, while young foals follow their long-maned mothers along narrow tracks between the purple patchwork.

Moorland climate is different: the air is noticeably softer and fresher, with sunlight enhancing the colours of the moor's muted palette. Even during the driest months bright green, mossy bogs remain squidgy and treacherous. Keeping an eye on the ground can be difficult when darkness descends, revealing a stunning star-studded sky - a cosmic spectacle as awe-inspiring today as it must have been to people in the distant past. On other nights, tumbling granite tors stand proud in the moonlight or can remain hidden for days, shrouded in swirling mist. Whatever the weather, in every season, Dartmoor captures the heart with its height and grandeur, its wildlife and its utter peace and solitude.

cuckoo. Birdsong steadily rises with the warmth and the summer months, but upland summers can be short. On the longest days the highest tors catch the first and last golden flare of sun, yet in the heat between dawn and dusk the hills sometimes vanish into purple haze. Then all that can be heard in the stillness is the faint murmur of a distant stream.

Summer transforms these uplands. When visitors crowd the car parks on busy weekends, the peace of the moor can still be found by walking just a few minutes away. Here buzzards

On the high moor, roads are few and far apart, often just a single lane with occasional passing places. They meander across the moor before diving deep into sparsely wooded valleys, crossing rivers over disconcertingly narrow medieval bridges. In a few places these structures provide a wider, surprisingly modern alternative to the precarious-looking old clapper bridge standing close by. History lies scattered across Dartmoor and evidence of human activity goes back over 10,000 years. First, Stone Age hunters tracked wild animals through the forest that once covered these uplands. Then Bronze Age settlers opened up the hills for farming, leaving a rich legacy of burial chambers, stone circles and menhirs littering the landscape, more than anywhere else in Europe. Iron Age and medieval communities followed, but as

the climate changed so too did the fate and fortunes of these moorland people.

In places modern tarmac is flanked by precariously balanced stone walls, some perhaps first placed by Bronze Age farmers, others constructed just a couple of centuries ago. Dartmoor's popularity continues to grow, and many of the centuries-old towns and villages have never been busier. Although offering opportunities for the local economy, the volume of people puts pressure on local amenities and a

Above: Wind-shaped, pony-pruned hawthorn at Combestone Tor.

Left: Bell heather and western gorse on the drier slopes.

Above: Buckland Beacon offers great views over the moors.

Facing page: The West Dart below Huccaby.

ating when bitterly cold, yet spellbinding when bathed in the warmth of the sun.

"If you can see the moors clearly it is going to rain. If you can't, it already is."

For the visitor who ventures out on to these uplands, Dartmoor is a chance to escape. For some it is their first opportunity, for others a regular event. They come for many reasons, perhaps to see if the place lives up to its picture-postcard image, or to discover if its sinister reputation painted so graphically in famous novels is true. However, most come simply to enjoy fresh air, to experience wildness and wide, open spaces, to wonder at the ancient granite piles and to wander over heather-clad hills.

Few places in our increasingly crowded isles offer such freedom of choice to hike unhindered so far and wide. Whether treading a pony track, following in the path of pre-historic people or striding across open moor, Dartmoor seldom disappoints. There is also increasing evidence that wild places such as this can be good for us; even simple outdoor activities such as a short stroll provide significant improvements in both health and quality of life. The greener, wilder and more peaceful the surroundings, the better the benefits - and Dartmoor always delivers.

conflict of interests as people vie to work or play. Today, Dartmoor is a microcosm of the challenges facing national parks nationwide - yet all agree this is a very special place.

Dartmoor stimulates the senses and satisfies the soul. The mere mention of the moor conjures a mixture of emotions: scary when cloaked in cloud, dismal when drenched, captiv-

1. Tors and torrents
Birth of the landscape

Sitting on the impressive granite stack of Haytor, making the most of a clear day on Dartmoor, you may well be forgiven for simply gazing at the magnificent views. Yet your cold stone seat has a dramatic story to tell.

Mountain building

Dartmoor is old, very old. The distinctive granite rock that underlies the moors has travelled far, not only from deep within the planet's molten core but also across the globe. At one time all the continents of the world lay close together and the south-west of England was submerged, part of a vast ocean basin located closer to the equator. From the adjacent land, rivers washed layer upon layer of sediments down to the sea. Coarse material was deposited in the deltas and shallows, eventually forming sandstone; finer material was carried into deeper water to form mudstone and shale. Over time, many of the ancient animals and plants trapped within these layers of sediment formed fossils. As the millennia passed, these submerged sediments were subsequently affected by intense heat and pressure that in places changed their character, distorting, fracturing and folding them.

Meanwhile, far below in the Earth's core, the furnaces of the Earth were stirring, rising closer to the surface.

Around 370 million years ago the area that was to become Devon and Cornwall lay under these warm, shallow seas - but this was soon to change. The continental plate upon which the sediments travelled crept north at the pace of the growth of a fingernail, around 2.5 centimetres a year. Submarine volcanoes became active, perhaps after passing over a thinner layer of crust, as seen in the region of the Hawaiian or Galapagos islands today. The first and oldest volcanic upwelling in the region lay beyond the Isles of Scilly, then five more great volcanic intrusions followed, causing molten lava to push up beneath the layers of sediments more than a mile thick. The resulting uplift built a great mountain chain that would shape the spine of the south-west of England. Some peaks probably reached up to 3,000 metres high, and Dartmoor was to be the youngest of these. Eventually the movement of magma ceased across the region. Around 280 million years ago, the molten lava cooled, cracked vertically and solidified to form one of the hardest rocks on earth - granite.

GRANITE

Granite consists of a groundmass of hard quartz, softer feldspar, biotite and mica. It is also characterised by a relatively high proportion of tourmaline, which is blacker than biotite and distinguished by its finely grooved surface. Three phases of fiery magma produced Dartmoor's characteristic rock, each one generating a slightly different type of granite. The first molten upwelling is thought to have produced the so-called 'giant' granite, with its distinctive large, whitish crystals. The second, finer 'blue' granite probably closely followed the first, and together these make up the most commonly found rocks. The third, the so-called 'contact' granite contaminated by minerals from the surrounding rocks, is finer still and much rarer.

Joints and faults

Contractions in the cooling granite created near-vertical fractures, and then hot water moving through these cracks led to some of them becoming lined or filled with minerals such as quartz or tourmaline, or both. Pressure in the Earth's crust controls the pattern of the joints, and movement along fault lines added to the fracturing.

Kaolin formation

Even some of the hardest materials can decompose in super-heated steam, permeating the rock by exploiting lines

Split granite reveals Dartmoor's distinctive giant feldspar in a matrix of grey quartz and other minerals.

An unusually large boulder of quartz-tourmaline, nearly half a metre across.

of weakness and eventually forming valuable deposits of kaolin or white clay. Today, China clay is still being extracted from places such as Lee Mill while the finer 'ball' clay, formed after being deposited in freshwater lakes, is mined in the Bovey basin.

subtropical forest, plant growth flourished in the heat and heavy rainfall. In these conditions, water and rotting vegetation formed acids that attacked and weakened the mineral found in granite known as feldspar, while the rock's more stable component, quartz, remained much less affected. Weathering took place along the lines of joints previously penetrated by water movement, and, where joints were close, the individual grains of granite became loosened, sometimes to great depths. Then, when exposed by further weathering and rock fall, the debris was washed away. However, the gradual erosion of Dartmoor granite over the following millennia was nothing compared to the next ordeal imposed by ice.

Ice Ages

Over the last two million years successive Ice Ages completed the final sculpting of Dartmoor's prominent peaks. Of perhaps twenty cold periods, on only four occasions did great ice sheets extend to cover most of the British Isles, none ever quite reaching southern England. Water continued to play a major part in shaping the granite tors, but this time by mechanical rather than chemical force.

This process began with a snowflake. Although it is hard to imagine that something so small and beautiful can be so destructive, when Arctic conditions stretched as far south as Dartmoor, winter snow could lie several metres deep, with

Today the West Dart below Two Bridges remains mainly ice free even in the coldest winters.

The top layers of softer sedimentary material quickly wore away to expose the hard volcanic roots of the mountains. Relieved of the weight, the granite expanded upward and fractured, forming horizontal joints following its surface. After the age of dinosaurs, some 60-30 million years ago, the great granite domes lay above sea level. Densely covered in devastating effects. Although massive ice sheets crushed the landscape further north, conditions on Dartmoor would have been more akin to the Arctic edge, with plant life sparse or nonexistent. However, while the surface snow melted seasonally, the stony ground below remained permanently frozen as much as several hundred metres deep. During the coldest months the lowest layers of snow, compressed by the weight above, turned to ice that penetrated the deepest rock fissures. Winters were long and summers were short. For tens of thousands of years, freezing was followed by thawing in the brief Arctic-like summers. The repeated expansion of ice and subsequent melting eventually prised the exposed rock sections apart to form the fractured tors we see today.

Gravity also played its part on these distinctive peaks. More falling snow added enough weight to start the frozen layers moving, dragging with them boulders as well as great blocks of granite. Most of the time the movement was slow as the rocks gradually crept downhill, sliding imperceptibly over frozen ground. Occasionally their descent was more dramatic when large sheets of ice crashed down the steepest slopes dragging debris and large boulders, along with thousands of tonnes of icc and snow, in a thundering, explosive avalanche. In this way, both slowly and catastrophically, massive slabs of rock were moved hundreds of metres. The result is a craggy, fractured granite peak surrounded by a boulder field of rock known as 'clitter' - a classic Dartmoor tor.

The tors

The word 'tor' is believed to come from the old Celtic name for a tower. Even on Dartmoor, rarely do massive lumps of exposed granite like Haytor grace prominent peaks, and few tors display the elegance and symmetry of Bellever. In academic circles the exact origin of granite tors has been hotly debated for centuries, perhaps because in global terms they are so rare. However, some experts have likened them to the 'kopje', granite outcrops that are found on the African plains.

Haytor is the most prominent and popular of all Dartmoor's massive granite heads.

Hound Tor
at sunset,
revealing jointed
blocks formed
by volcanic
force and ice.

OTHER ROCKS AND MINERALS FOUND ON DARTMOOR

Other rocks of volcanic origin occur within the National Park. Dolerite is quarried commercially for road stone and railway ballast at Meldon Quarry, Crockam Quarry and Pitts Cleave, all now designated as Sites of Special Scientific Interest.

Dartmoor is also rich in rare metals and other minerals. For over four thousand years people attempted to mine the mineral wealth of the moors, searching stream beds, digging holes and sinking shafts with varying success. Tin was once a major export and for a while in the 1860s Dartmoor had the largest copper mine in the world. Arsenic was produced in some quantity and smaller finds were made of lead, silver and even minuscule amounts of gold.

Everyone seems to have their own favourite tor. While Haytor is impressive, its rounded appearance does not compare to the unruly ruggedness of Hound Tor or Honeybag Tor. Features of individual rocks have also sparked lively debates in the past. Weathering can give rise to smooth, bowl-like depressions in horizontal granite surfaces. Far from a man-made origin for a long lost ritual, these rock basins are thought to have formed by the repeated freezing and expansion of ice that progressively prised out individual mineral grains. The resulting hollow space can hold water in winter, yet quickly dries in warm weather.

Not all the summits consist of granite. The famous landmark of Brent Tor, with its hilltop church on the western edge of the moor, is formed from an undersea lava flow of some 350 million years ago. This is remarkable in that volcanic submarine flows of this kind usually result in pillow lava, not in the accumulations of unsorted glassy, rock fragments as found at Brent Tor.

Torrents

Dartmoor is broadly divided in two. Sloping slightly from north to south, its larger northern plateau and smaller southern plateau are separated by a central basin. The natural drainage from the high ground feeds nearly all of Devon's main rivers. Five of them even originate just a short walk from each other yet flow in opposite directions, heading for different coasts. All are undoubtedly picturesque, but the River Dart is the most famous and its two main sources join at the aptly named Dartmeet.

River valleys were carved deep into the moorland edge over great periods of time. Around 14,000 years ago the last Ice

Age began to end, and this occurred surprisingly quickly. Spring started to arrive earlier and day by day the sky grew brighter, the air warmer. The snow disappeared and the permafrost soon followed. Without so much reflective white, the darker ground absorbed more heat and warmed faster.

The rapidly rising spring temperatures unleashed meltwater from the once permanently frozen ground. Cascading down through steep-sided gorges, the deluge destroyed everything in its path, carrying away rocks deposited by thousands of years of ice and snow movement. These rivers were wider, faster and more destructive than anything we would see today. At the time, these rivers also had further to travel to the sea. When Britain was still joined to the continent by land, sea levels were perhaps 50 metres lower than at present and the English Channel was a vast valley through which a great river flowed, fed by the modern-day Thames and Rhine. As a result, even exceptional downpours by today's standards pale into insignificance when compared to the torrents of the past. Such floods must have happened many times over the Ice Ages, deepening the valleys time and time again.

A jumble of granite boulders line the bed of today's moorland rivers, dumped by fast-flowing spates in the aftermath of the Ice Ages as the water level eventually fell and slowed. Today, in the blissful warmth of summer, watching sparkling clear water swirling gently around large rocks and over rounded stones, it is a reminder that once far greater forces were at work.

Bench Tor sits high above the deeply carved valley downstream of Dartmeet.

Sticklepath Fault

Rivers exploit the landscape in their headlong dash to the sea. Granite is hard, not easily eroded by streams and rivers, yet sometimes volcanic forces provide a ready-made passage. A buzzard's eye view across eastern Dartmoor

DARTMOOR MAROONED

Perhaps one of Dartmoor's most bizarre moments in prehistory is when it briefly became an island. Around 2.5 million years ago sea levels rose dramatically, drowning huge areas of the surrounding land, leaving Dartmoor marooned. Evidence for this extraordinary event can still best be seen in the wave-cut platforms and reefs once fashioned by prevailing winds and waves pounding into the south-west side of the moor.

reveals a massive rift cutting across the plateau. This is the telltale sign of a fault, a substantial crack in the Earth's crust that was created around 60 million years ago.

This huge scar, known as the Sticklepath Fault, crosses the entire south-west peninsula, often forming a deep valley. The Fault literally tears the county of Devon in two, from Torquay to Torrington and beyond, passing out across the Bristol Channel north of Lundy island. Over time this rift has been used as a channel by various rivers, and now accommodates the Bovey and tributaries of the Taw and Teign.

Peat

Between Ice Ages Dartmoor was certainly more hospitable, but the high moor was still a tough place for plants to survive in almost sub-Arctic conditions. Heather covered the drier ground, while mosses massed only in the wettest places. Here, the cold, damp, acidic conditions produced a soil of partially decayed vegetation known as peat. Today, over a third of all the unenclosed moorland on Dartmoor is covered by peat that measures over half a metre thick in depth; in places it is considerably deeper, perhaps 7 metres or more. This peat forms the vast blanket bogs at the heart of the high moor as well as the mires of the lower valleys. However, it is no longer accumulating, most probably because it formed under much wetter conditions than those of the present day.

Peat was once important as a fuel for burning. Crucially for us, it also helps the moor to act like a giant sponge, providing a vital water-holding resource for the entire county. Now scientific research has given peat a new importance, revealing remarkable detail about the past climate and vegetation of Dartmoor from studies of the substance's preserved pollen.

So Dartmoor is the product of molten rock and mountain building, wind and water, ice and fire. And, last but not least, the impact of generations of people.

Facing page: The River Dart below Hexworthy bridge runs fast and deep.

An ancient cairn
on Rippon Tor has
panoramic views
towards Haytor
and Hound Tor.

2. Rock and roll
The uses of granite

Handled and hauled, manoeuvred and lifted by people for thousands of years, Dartmoor granite was first used not for houses but for ritual and ceremony. Neolithic people erected stones and stood them in rows, constructed elaborate chambered tombs and capped burial sites with great slabs. Only later as trees became scarce was granite used to build the walls of Bronze Age roundhouses. From medieval days to modern times farmers cleared the rocks from their land. They used the granite for their buildings and boundary stones, as well as for walls, gateposts and stiles. Marker posts were erected to guide them in the mist, and bridges to cross raging streams.

The arrival of iron tools meant that the hard, quartz-rich rock could more easily be carved and shaped into everyday tools and utensils. Breaking, pounding and grinding by hardy, highly skilled quarrymen fashioned granite for all manner of useful purposes. The techniques for splitting and shaping large stones changed little through the ages, using wedges and chisels to form animal drinking troughs, mill stones and rollers. In cider presses, granite was used to pulp the apples and channelled troughs of the stone collected the juice. Stamping mills crushed tin ore before smelting, and it was granite that often formed the foundations for the machinery that powered the Industrial Revolution.

A skillfully hewn granite sink on a Dartmoor farm was used to wash clothes.

A typical Dartmoor granary and farm outbuildings constructed of granite.

Over millennia, despite changes in culture and religious belief, many communities used granite in the same way. Of all monuments the simple monolith still links ancient and modern people - from Neolithic standing stones to machine-polished memorials for more recent fallen heroes. Over the last few centuries Dartmoor granite has travelled far and wide, throughout Britain and far beyond, and has been used to construct grand houses, forts, prisons, museums, bridges, breakwaters, dams, dockyards and lighthouses. Its enduring qualities made it the stone of choice for the architects of some of England's finest buildings, including the Liverpool Slave Market and, in London, Nelson's Column, the National

The remains of lifting gear still lie in the long-abandoned Haytor Quarry.

Rock-carved rails built in 1820 once carried wagonloads of granite down to barges.

Gallery, parts of the British Museum and the old General Post Office, as well as London Bridge, although the last-mentioned is now to be found relocated to Arizona.

The granite tramway

The ingenuity of the quarrymen who toiled to transport the rock left some intriguing legacies of their industry. One of the most fascinating begins near Haytor where a granite tramway was laid with substantial stone rails built into the moorland. Wagons pulled by teams of horses heaved the heavy stone down to the Stover Canal and along the Teign estuary by barge to begin its long journey to London.

Facing page: St Raphael's Church, Huccaby. Granite is so tough it was difficult to work without metal tools.

3. Wet and wild
Climate and people shaping the landscape

If we think the Dartmoor of today is sometimes a little bleak, spare a thought for the first nomadic hunters who wandered this way at the end of the last Ice Age. Clothed in furs from head to toe and armed with spears, bows and arrows, these early Stone Age people would have walked across a barren, still partially frozen, landscape - a place more Svalbard than South Devon. The sound of scrunching gravel underfoot would have accompanied a small party such as this, because the land had been all but wiped clean of ground cover by a hundred-thousand years of sub-Arctic weather. The tors were recognisable by then, and so too the rivers, running lower, as the meltwater torrents had largely subsided.

Plant life then was scarce; the reindeer that the hunters probably pursued scraped a living from the lichen and mosses struggling to grow on these desolate, rocky uplands. Here, varying shades of grey granite and pools of water gave light relief to the surroundings. Only algae formed dark patches snaking down hillsides in the occasional damp, solid stream of gravel and stony silt. Yet splashes of colour may have brightened the Stone Age view; it is possible that scattered tufts of alpine flowers survived the icy conditions, spreading and declining as the climate cycled from warm to freezing, and back again.

People and the landscape

Prehistoric people must have periodically visited the uplands of Dartmoor; after all, we know they were not too far away. They left tools in Kent's Cavern on the South Devon coast throughout the last three glaciations and the warmer times in between. Among the most spectacular finds in this cave was a reindeer antler fashioned into a spear tip, dated to around 15,000 years ago. The hunters' successors would have surely noticed the climate changing as the last Ice Age lurched to an end just a few hundred years later.

From examination of Greenland ice cores we have also now learned that average temperatures at that time rocketed by 12°C in less than two human generations. This effectively ended the freezing conditions for a short time, but the warmth was short-lived. Temperatures suddenly plunged again before finally starting to warm a few thousand years

Facing page: Partial thawing and re-freezing forms icicle cascades down a rock face.

Free of permanent ice cover, plant life was quick to return. Dwarf willow and birch scrub soon colonised thin pockets of soil, then heather, sedge and grass arrived too. Eventually these pioneering plants were followed by trees, mainly birch and then pine. The strength of the wind that brought in the first seeds steadily declined and rainfall increased. By 7,000 years ago denser woodland had spread up the valleys, dominated by hazel and oak with some elm, along with alder in the wetter sites. The landscape was transformed - in just a few millennia the tundra had given way to trees, Britain had become an island, and Dartmoor a forest.

The patchy green woodland canopy covering all but the highest tors thrived for a few thousand years until the arrival of new, more industrious people. Bronze Age settlers built their roundhouses, systematically divided the land among them, and no doubt discussed Dartmoor's fickle weather just as much as we do today. But warmer or drier, cooler or wetter, past climates played a major part in dictating the destiny of moorland communities. From around 4,500 years ago increasing human activity was evident, with widespread fires man-made as well as natural. The burning, whether started by lightning strike or deliberately, destroyed large parts of the remaining forest and opened up the high moor to heather once again. Woodland survived mainly around the moorland edge and in rock-strewn river valleys.

Dating from 1300 BC, a granite wall at Grimspound encircled 24 roundhouses.

later. Rather alarmingly, the reorganisation of Atlantic weather that triggered these incredible changes seems to have occurred in just a couple of years, and the impact of this warming was dramatic.

As time marched on, Iron Age hill forts started to appear on the margins of the moor. Although Dartmoor was warmer and drier for much of the Roman occupation, the legions apparently ignored these uplands in their haste to exploit Cornish tin and other minerals. When the Dark Ages descended following the Roman withdrawal, Celtic Devon may not have been as 'dark' as the rest of Britain. In 2001, new findings emerged from the sixth century, at the time King Arthur was rumoured to have reigned. The discovery suggests that perhaps wealthy Devonians were then holding 'beach parties' with Byzantine merchants. At the mouth of one river on the South Devon coast they appear to have regularly traded Dartmoor tin for Mediterranean wine brought in by trading ships.

Anglo-Saxons populated the more productive moorland valleys, and medieval villages grew as fast on the moor as elsewhere in Britain. William the Conqueror made the whole of Devon a Royal Forest, a great hunting ground for his Norman noblemen. When King John came to the throne he retained only the uplands for his sport. Later his son gave it away but the Crown subsequently regained it, and in 1337 Edward III granted Dartmoor to his son, elevated him to the position of a Duke, and so created the Duchy of Cornwall that today still owns a large part of the moor.

DARTMOOR CLIMATE

"Why wait for an entire year? On Dartmoor you can experience all four seasons in a single day."

The south-west of England boasts an enviable record for the mildest climate in Britain. Dartmoor is different, being cooler and wetter. Being so high, it catches the worst of the weather sweeping in from the Atlantic. Average annual rainfall over the high north moors reaches over 2.5 metres and, in some exceptional years, over 3 metres of rain has been recorded. When compared to the south coast around Exmouth, which barely gets 750mm of rain a year, parts of Dartmoor are positively drenched.

Moorland temperatures, too, are well below the region's annual average. Princetown is around 3°C less than the coast, which at a comparatively balmy 11°C is close to the mean sea temperature. In contrast winters can be cold; -9°C is not unknown, and when wind chill is added conditions can become dangerous.

An aerial view of Fox Tor Mire, with old tin workings in the foreground.

The birth of bog

The River Dart begins its journey to the English Channel, not bubbling enticingly from a hillside spring, but oozing quietly from a treacherous, sodden mass known as a bog. And it is not alone - most of Devon's major rivers trickle from the same bog. The Okement and Taw, Teign, Tavy and Dart, along with perhaps a hundred lesser streams, all seep from the plateau north of the Moretonhampstead-to-Princetown road.

Today, the central high ground of Dartmoor has an almost sub-Arctic altitude, with heavy rainfall and relatively impervious rock close to the surface. In the past, when warmer and wetter, these were the vital ingredients for bog formation, creating the cool, acidic conditions necessary for a special moss to thrive - sphagnum, the bog maker. The biggest bogs can be measured in square miles, while a small wet hollow can become the site for a bog not much bigger than a bush hat. A different type of bog can also be found in the valleys - known as a mire.

Blanket bogs

The two biggest bogs by far could perhaps be better described as wet moorland. The largest covers the northern plateau and the area around Cranmere Pool can be difficult to cross, but Rayharrow Pool is one of the few really dangerous bogs on Dartmoor and is best avoided. Other notorious bogs can be

AVOIDING A STICKY END

The best advice to avoid coming to a sticky end in a bog is to follow pony tracks. A well-known saying is that 'Dartmoor ponies only go where tussocks grow'. Leaping from one grassy tussock to another across a small bog is a wonderful childhood sport. Only later in life does one discover that this is also where venomous adders often bask in dry summer weather.

found on the southern plateau; from this slightly lower blanket bog weep the rivers Avon, Plym, Erme and Swincombe, an area that is home to two potentially perilous bogs. Fox Tor Mire is perhaps better known as the scary Grimpen Mire of

Sherlock Holmes fame, while the smaller but still equally treacherous Red Lake Mire should only be approached with the greatest respect and care. Despite local legends to the contrary, no bog is bottomless, but in places they may be several metres deep.

Valley mires

Around the margin of the moor where rivers drain from the central high ground another type of bog exists. Most of this kind seem to form where the steepness of the slope slackens around the 365-metre contour; this is actually the height of an ancient shore line cut into the granite surface. Here rivers naturally pause, depositing silt before continuing their downward journey to the sea. As the stream beds wander off-course and the vegetation grows and decays over the centuries, the floor of this basin becomes filled with a light and spongy peat, held together by a growing mat of roots from above. Where water continues to flow underneath, a mossy mound rises to form an unstable bright green carpet, wobbling and swaying unnervingly if any attempt is made to walk across it.

Heath

Drier areas of moor rank among the most attractive places to visit in late summer. From July to September the sight and smell of heather transforms vast swathes of uplands. Infrequent controlled burning, known as 'swaling' on Dartmoor, clears areas of tall gorse scrub and allows the heather space to grow. Burn too often and only grasses and bracken can thrive.

Oak woodland

The extensive oak woodland that once dominated Dartmoor's widespread forest is now largely confined to steep river corridors and gentler valleys, the exceptions to this being the isolated, eerie remnants clustered in remote copses such as Wistman's Wood, Black Tor Beare and Piles Copse. First impressions reinforce their legendary status; they appear more 'bonsai' than big.

Wistman's Wood is the most accessible of these copses to reach, and contains the most twisted and stunted trees. Yet their growth between large granite boulders makes the woodland difficult to enter. This copse is one of the most spectacular in Britain for its wealth of mosses, liverworts, lichens and ferns, many draping from its weird and wonderfully warped trunks and contorted branches. The oaks themselves seldom reach more than 4 metres high - yet, far from being some special, upland variety, these trees are all common English oak.

Why they have survived in this spot when all others on the moor have vanished is complex, and various theories and explanations abound. Perhaps they were spared centuries of fire and axe by their remoteness, or were sheep and ponies unable to gain easy access over the rocks to nibble new growth, or did superstition help? Much more likely is that it is a combination of factors. The most plausible theory is that the contorted shapes were a product of centuries of branch lopping by scavenging miners to fuel Dartmoor's tin industry. Whatever the cause, it now seems that only a few trees live more than a century up here, the oldest being barely more than 300 years old. Indeed, monitoring since the 1950s suggests that some of these relic, high-altitude woods may today be expanding, and new trunks growing straighter.

Not all of Dartmoor's leafy woodlands look the same during the warmer months. At Steps Bridge near Dunsford on the River Teign, a special nature reserve of woodland is managed by the Devon Wildlife Trust and celebrates spring with an annual spectacle of wild daffodils. A different colour heralds the start of summer in other woods - Wray Cleave is renowned for its bluebells, as are the woodlands above Okehampton.

Coniferous plantation

When Neolithic settlers on the moors first built chambered tombs some 5,000 years ago, trees may still have graced the skyline. But for the last few millennia the high moor has basked under open skies - that was until the first conifer plantations appeared in the late 1700s. Early plantings consisted of Scots pine, European larch and Norway spruce, often mixed with oak, beech or sycamore. Only since the First World War have other bigger, darker, denser blocks of conifers - mainly exotic Sitka and Norway spruce, Douglas fir and Japanese larch - been systematically planted. Many were laid out with reckless disregard for historically important sites such as ancient homes and old stone walls. In these more enlightened times, the sound of chain saws echoing in the plantations has seen some conifers clear-felled and not replaced.

Wistman's wood is the best-known upland oak wood found above 250 metres on Dartmoor.

High humidity favours ferns, mosses and lichens, enabling them to grow on Dartmoor trees.

Wet woodland

Few trees flourish with their roots in soggy soil, but here willow and alder abound, lining stream sides in valley bottoms and around some mires. Willow especially can be found surprisingly high on the moor, forming small clumps far from other woodland, often around old mineral workings. Willow has its uses, once being valuable for brooms, baskets and even the manufacture of clogs.

Parkland, coppice and orchard

For hundreds of years people have played with the landscape around their homes to improve productivity or enhance the aspect. Deer parks became an essential feature of great estates from Norman to Georgian times, as much for meat as for their scenic beauty. The Victorians then made parklands fashionable for a show of wealth, a place to grow exotic trees from seeds brought home by plant hunters visiting distant corners of the globe. Old deer parks can still be found at Okehampton, Whiddon near Castle Drogo, Blatchford near Cornwood, Holne near Ashburton and Parke at Bovey Tracey. The lush grasslands of these parks are now more often grazed by sheep and cattle than deer, beneath their scattering of majestic specimen trees.

Planted hazel coppice became common in medieval times, providing fuel for burning, poles for tool handles and sticks for thatching spars, along with many other uses. Hazel grows naturally with oak and people in the past exploited this natural preference, realising the potential of cutting hazel every seven years or so to create a sustainable crop. The hazel forms an understorey, forcing the oak to grow taller to seek better light, that in turn produces straighter oak trunks.

The Dunsford Nature Reserve alongside the Teign river is famed for its wild daffodils.

Devon is justly famous for its cider orchards. Before the days of reliably clean drinking water, alcohol produced from naturally fermenting apple juice made cider a safe, nutritious drink. This beverage once even formed part of a farm worker's daily pay. Over many centuries, in almost every suitable Dartmoor valley, late summer found apple trees groaning under the weight of juicy, ripening fruit. Sharp, acidic cider apples. It was a harvest waiting to be turned into the county's legendary amber nectar, which some say has the power to launch rockets - otherwise known as scrumpy.

Harsh winter
weather and
acid soil limits
the growth of
trees on the
high moor.

4. Standing stones and summer homes
A remarkable heritage

For a rare glimpse into a lost world, long gone but not entirely vanished, few places in the world boast so many prehistoric relics as Dartmoor. Today the National Park

The Merrivale stone rows are some of the most important Bronze Age relics on Dartmoor.

contains the greatest concentration of Bronze Age remains in Britain, and the most significant in the whole of Europe. The reason for the continued existence of so many ancient homes and ritual sites is partly because they were built of granite, one of nature's most durable rocks. In addition, later human activity on the moor was not as intensive as on the surrounding lowlands - ploughs and hard rock do not mix well.

Sadly for any budding Indiana Jones, or those who have made a career from digging and delving into evidence of people of the past, the high soil acidity means that virtually no prehistoric pottery, bone or metal survives on the moor. It is fortunate, therefore, that today all remaining monuments are protected by law, making it an offence to damage or interfere with them.

The earliest remains

Early Mesolithic or Middle Stone Age people left behind only a few flint weapons and tools, evidence of their hunting

and gathering lifestyle scattered on the fringes of the moor. During their travels in search of food, these people collected all they needed from the natural world - wood, stone, animal skins, sinew and antler. Few visible relics can be dated to before 4,300 years ago, yet those that do were built to impress. Neolithic or New Stone Age earth burial mounds, and even rarer stone chambers, still exist in surprisingly good condition. Here human bones were once laid to rest with the greatest respect.

During the Neolithic period, around 4500-2300 BC, a more settled way of life began to emerge. In the surrounding lowlands the first farmsteads appeared, crops were planted and animals domesticated. Then, in the later Neolithic and early Bronze Age periods, lasting from 2300 to 700 BC in Britain, people constructed an intriguing variety of ceremonial structures on the moor, a type rarely found outside Britain and Ireland.

This was the age of mysterious stone rows and circles, raised by ancient peoples who buried their dead beneath mounds of stone. At first interments tended to be communal; only later were the dead individually laid in rock-built cists and cairns. This was probably a practical precaution as well as one of spiritual significance. The building of sturdy round-houses and high farm walls around the same time suggest defensive measures may have been needed to protect

against scavengers such as bulldozing wild boar and marauding wolves and bears.

Spread of farmland

The arrival of 'Beaker' people, so named after their distinctive pottery, revolutionised post-Stone-Age Britain. With them came a talented elite, special people who were perhaps thought to possess supernatural powers. They had learnt to smelt copper and the rarer tin together to produce an even harder metal - bronze. From liquid fire they could conjure a sharp-edged axe; this was soon followed by the sword, a weapon representing the cutting edge of technology at the time. Although some of the first bronze in the British Isles

The Bronze Age remains of at least 36 round-houses and four enclosures survive at Merrivale.

BRONZE AGE FARMSTEADS

On Dartmoor over 5,000 Bronze Age buildings, known as roundhouses, survive – although only the granite walls remain today. Generally circular, these buildings measure anything from 1.8 to 9 metres in diameter. Sometimes the large upright stones framing the door-way can still be seen as some even had porches to protect the entrance from the wind and rain.

The roof timbers were supported by a ring of posts inside the wall, giving the roof a conical shape that was then covered by turf, heather, gorse or thatch, whatever was readily available. The interior of Bronze Age roundhouses were designed for open-plan living – space for a family to cook, eat and sleep, and perhaps even room for a crude loom to weave cloth. A central open fire provided heat for cooking and warmth in winter. These roundhouses continued to be built and lived in throughout the Iron Age.

Bronze Age people divided their land with low walls that we now call reaves; these can best be seen from a distance, looking from one hillside to another. Mostly the low banks run in parallel lines down valley slopes, dividing the land into narrow strips.

Bronze age reaves mark prehistoric field boundaries above the Dart valley near Dartmeet.

was made from Irish copper and Cornish tin, it was not long before both were probably discovered around Dartmoor.

By the middle Bronze Age, around 3,700 years ago, farmland had replaced forest on the high moor. Celtic culture had spread across the British Isles and the weather was warmer and drier than the present day. The prehistoric farmers of Dartmoor built some of Britain's first fields - long strips of land surrounded by low stone banks known as 'reaves'. Within these walls, crops were grown and animals grazed.

The farmers lived close by, sometimes in a single roundhouse within a field, or clustered together in an unenclosed settlement similar to a modern village. Evidence also suggests that some of these farmers may not have lived on the moor all year round, perhaps just driving their cattle and sheep from the lowlands to the higher ground for summer grazing.

Life appears to have been relatively peaceful in the Bronze Age, and that transformed the growing communities. More permanent homes and villages evolved; neighbours were a novelty, and then became common. In just a few hundred years Britain experienced a population boom and expanded to perhaps half a million inhabitants. Domestic life was at the heart of everything these people did and no doubt alliances, formed by marriage between families, set the pattern for our modern society.

Rise of the hill fort

Towards the end of the Bronze Age the climate started to cool and rainfall increased. Wetter conditions meant soils became more acid, and grass and crops no longer thrived. The attraction of Dartmoor for farming waned with the weather. Gradually the burial places of ancestors were deserted, fields left fallow and buildings abandoned, as the previous inhabitants moved to the lowlands.

The Iron Age, from 700 BC until the arrival of the Romans in Britain in the first century AD, saw more troubled times, even in the depths of Devon. The arrival of harder, sharper weapons saw society descend into violence. Within a few hundred years in southern Britain, young men began to earn status in battle and a new class of social elite emerged - the warrior. At around the same time the first real evidence of widespread horse riding elevated warfare to a new, brutal level.

While few people continued to live on the exposed high moor, some farmers remained in roundhouses situated on the lower slopes. But the danger of attack from neighbouring tribes brought about the need for better defences, and a new age of large-scale earthwork construction subsequently saw the development of hill forts, protected by ramparts and wooden palisades. By 75 BC, in the late Celtic Iron Age, society

HILL FORTS

Twelve hill forts are known to lie within the National Park. Clustered with commanding views over the Teign valley, the three most notable of these forts can be seen at Prestonbury, Cranbrook and Wooston. On the south-east edge of Dartmoor, with its deep ditches and high ramparts, Hembury Hill Fort is one of the finest examples.

was deeply divided. Kings were at the top, slaves at the bottom - yet perhaps the druids, with their mistletoe and golden sickles, held the real power, even capable of stopping battles.

Around AD 50 the Roman army reached Exeter as they continued their conquest of Britain. Occupying a commanding position that overlooked the River Exe, they built a fortress on a spur that became the base for the 5,000-strong Second Augustan Legion. Yet, despite the Romans' views of Dartmoor in the distance, only a few scattered hoards of their coins have ever been discovered on the moors. The Romans also established two smaller forts on the northern fringes of Dartmoor, one at North Tawton and the other at Okehampton, a signal-tower at Sourton and a fortlet at Ide. Dartmoor itself appears to have been a largely Roman-free zone.

The Dartmoor longhouse

Some 600 years after the last Roman legion had sailed from Britain's shores, the Normans invaded, and with them came a new style of living. Not long after William had subdued the Saxons, the traditional rectangular Dartmoor longhouse began to appear, built on a slope with thick granite walls and a heavily thatched roof.

The first longhouses were single-storey buildings with a central hearth but no chimney; the smoke simply worked its way out through the roof covering. The upper part of the

Right: The animal house at Uppacott is virtually unchanged since medieval times.

Facing page: Uppacott is a superb example of an early Devon longhouse.

house was used by humans, the lower part by cattle, and the two sections were separated by a cross passage. Heat from the farm animals helped keep the people warm and the downhill drainage allowed the muck to flow in the opposite direction, out through a small hole in the bottom wall.

Industrial construction

Many present-day settlements on the moor owe their origins to medieval builders; almost as many again now lie deserted.

From the Middle Ages to later times, central Dartmoor was used for industry as well as farming. Tin ore was extensively mined, crushed and smelted from the twelfth century, leaving a lumpy legacy of miners' hard labour. Over time, numerous more modern quarries became derelict as demand for the rock declined. Today, among the rubble of their old workings, large slabs still remain where they fell, often with lines of drilled holes revealing the method used for splitting.

Peat was once an important fuel for heating the home and cooking. Even today old peat workings still catch the occasional unwary walker, soaking shoes and trousers. So too do the diggings of some of the country's first rabbit warrens. Farmed for their fur and flesh, the creatures were imported from France and first mentioned in the Isles of Scilly in 1137. Sometime later they began to appear on Dartmoor, and it was not long before rabbits became big business on the moor. They were kept in specially built mounds, contained by stone walls and surrounded by vermin traps to reduce predation by stoat, and even polecat. This industry inevitably led to the unleashing of a nibbling horde across Britain as rabbits escaped and established wild colonies.

Water is Dartmoor's biggest export; eight reservoirs were built between 1861 and 1972. Before that, a complex series of carefully constructed channels known as leats were built to follow the moorland contours and carry water to power industrial machinery and supply farms. A major leat was even built in Tudor times to supply the city of Plymouth. When Sir Francis Drake became Mayor of Plymouth in 1581, water was needed for naval and merchant ships, so he initiated the construction of 'Drake's Leat' just a decade later.

The military themselves added a new chapter to moorland archaeology in the nineteenth century as they began to use the land for training. Today, their red flags signal the danger zones, while many observation posts, target tramways and slit trenches mark parts of the north moor landscape.

Various attempts to farm the open moors again were made at least two centuries before William the Conqueror arrived. Since then new farms have been built and old ones restored, land has been cleared for fields, and overgrown areas have been irregularly reclaimed. Upland farming is a fickle business at the best of times and many ventures now lie neglected, not for the first time.

The history of human endeavour on Dartmoor is perhaps more impressive because so many massive structures survive. Far from leaving just the odd boundary, building or stone tool, here generations of people worked and worshipped, fought and farmed, struggled and thrived - leaving a remarkably rich and visible heritage of the coming of civilisation to the British Isles.

Dawn at Kennick Reservoir. It was the second of its kind to be built on Dartmoor, in 1884.

MUDDY REVELATIONS

Seldom has the draining of a reservoir for routine maintenance caused so much excitement. When the waters of Tottiford Reservoir on Dartmoor were lowered in autumn 2009, a previously unknown prehistoric complex emerged from the mud. The reservoir was the first to be built on the moor, and stone rows, burial cairns and a stone circle had been hidden beneath it since 1861.

Mike Miller from nearby Moretonhampstead first spotted the significance of the site. He contacted Jane Marchand, Senior Archaeologist with Dartmoor National Park Authority, reporting that he had noticed two stone rows and some burial cairns in the reservoir's basin. Further visits to Tottiford confirmed the findings that later led to the discovery of a large 22-metre stone circle by Channel 4's *Time Team*. Tony Robinson and his group of experts descended on the site with Jane Marchand, who commented at the time:

> "The location of this site on the most eastern spur of Dartmoor is particularly interesting as this is an area with little recorded prehistoric archaeology compared to the rest of the moor. There was no knowledge of the existence of this complex as the reservoir's construction pre-dates the beginning of systematic archaeological recording on Dartmoor.

In total the ceremonial complex consists of a free-standing stone circle, a double stone row and single stone row, with regularly spaced stones and which both seem to end on burial cairns. There are at least eight other cairns within the area. It is believed that the complex is at least 4,000 years old and its discovery has to rank as one of the most important on Dartmoor in recent times."

So the archaeological dig could take place in August 2010, South West Water lowered the levels again by transferring the water into the neighbouring Trenchford Reservoir. A 60-strong team and television crew spent three days investigating the reservoir bed. The dig confirmed the prehistoric origins of the site and added some intriguing detail.

At the time Jim Mower, *Time Team*'s Development Producer, reported: "We had a fantastic shoot and everyone on the team thought the site was exciting and interesting. We are confident that an excellent programme will result. None of this would have been possible without the enthusiasm and assistance of South West Water. We have never had a reservoir drained before for one of our programmes! I hope we've been able to make a lasting contribution to the archaeology of Dartmoor National Park."

Tottiford Reservoir was the first to be built, in 1861, flooding a previously unrecognised prehistoric site.

Jane Marchand confirmed: "Some finely worked flint tools were also found close to the complex; these included knives, piercers, notched blades, microliths (very small flint tools used as barbs, tips of arrows, or placed edge-to-edge in a wooden haft) and some cores (the remains of a flint nodule from which the tools were made). Some of the tools date back to Mesolithic times around 8,000 years ago, indicating that this area has been the focus of human activity over many millennia."

Armchair archaeologists across the nation watched enthralled as the muddy revelations of this prime time documentary were revealed. The film crew's visit was their two-hundredth programme, a timely return to the county that hosted the first-ever *Time Team* dig. Tottiford turned out to be an impressive natural amphitheatre, used by ancient people. The area was surveyed and preliminary geophysical work carried out, before the site once again disappeared beneath the reservoir water.

5. The National Park
The creation and cultivation of a national icon

In the early 1800s the romantic poetry of Byron, Coleridge and Wordsworth, to name just a few, inspired a movement that changed the way people perceived and enjoyed the great outdoors. Until then the wild, most remote parts of Britain were seen as positively perilous and uncultured. Waxing lyrical about the 'untamed' countryside, Wordsworth famously claimed the Lake District to be 'a sort of national property, in which every man has a right and an interest who has an eye to perceive and a heart to enjoy'. Surprisingly, poets helped to change the way people saw the world about them, though it was to be the visionary Scotsman, John Muir, who inspired the establishment of the world's first national park in 1872 - Yellowstone, in North America.

Birth of the National Park

Facing page: Enjoyment and appreciation of nature is a vital part of the National Park purpose.

Around half a century later in Britain, a growing appreciation for the nation's landscape, along with the perceived benefits of regular exercise, a sense of freedom and a widespread spiritual revival, led to demands for more access to the countryside. The unprecedented expansion of towns and cities, at a time when landowners continued to deny entry to their properties because of intensive agriculture or sporting activities, led to increasing conflict - even a mass trespass in April 1932 in the Peak District. In Devon, discussion around Dartmoor becoming a national park was almost stopped before it could begin. However, a regional newspaper stoked the argument when it printed a quote from a major West Country landowner in 1929: "'The probability of Dartmoor ever becoming a National Park is exceedingly remote,' our London correspondent writes."

The deliberations concluded in 1949 when an Act of Parliament established national parks in Britain - across the country the race was immediately on. Dartmoor was to become one of the first national parks and was formally created on 30 October 1951, the fourth to be designated this status in a matter of months. The new national park then covered an area of some 365 square miles, from Okehampton to Ivybridge and from Tavistock to Bovey Tracey. And it included much more than just high moorland - farmland, gorges, river valleys and woods all rich in wildlife and archaeology were included within its new borders.

'Parke' is the headquarters of the Dartmoor National Park Authority.

Managing Dartmoor National Park

Strangely, the archives of local plans in Devon for the great inauguration day seem remarkably subdued and some personal memories from the time recollect the event was without any great ceremony or emotion. In comparison with the public debate and establishment of later national parks in Sussex, Hampshire and Scotland, the local response at the time does appear astonishingly restrained.

The first meeting of the Dartmoor National Park Committee was held on 19 February 1952. This committee comprised twelve County Councillors and six Members appointed by the National Parks Commission. Alderman Hayter Hames CBE, JP was elected Chairman and four other aldermen,

three JPs, two CBEs, two DSOs, two Lt Colonels, two Majors, one Professor, a Lord, a Lady and two Knights filled the ranks. Of all the great and good, one member of this committee was to stand out from the others on numerous occasions. The innocent-sounding Lady Sylvia Sayer became an ardent early conservator of Dartmoor National Park. It was alleged that just the mere mention of her name could make the highest park official turn pale. She was fearless and passionate in her personal mission to defend Dartmoor, even once deliberately interrupting military live firing on the north moor. More famously, Lady Sayer once snubbed the Duke of Cornwall when Duchy management plans agreed to continued manoeuvres on the moor by the armed forces.

For the first four-and-a-half decades of its existence the aforementioned committee administered Dartmoor. Then in 1997, Dartmoor National Park became a free-standing local authority, bound by various Acts of Parliament and governed by 22 appointed members - they include many local councillors and members representing various aspects of Dartmoor life. The local authority was charged with a duty to conserve and enhance the natural beauty, wildlife and cultural heritage of Dartmoor, while promoting opportunities for the understanding and enjoyment of the special qualities of the National Park by the public. It was also charged with fostering the economic and social well being of the communities within its boundaries. Considering that Dartmoor has a population of more than 34,000 residents and many millions of day visitors a year, added to that the odd moorland fire and occasional severe blizzard, along with a wide diversity of activities and interests taking place within its boundaries, the sheer challenge of managing the Park becomes apparent.

Today, the headquarters of Dartmoor National Park is situated on the outskirts of Bovey Tracey at a property named Parke. Owned by the National Trust, the house and stables is leased to the Authority while the grounds remain open to the public. The Hole family completed the present-day mansion in 1828 on the site of a former fortified manor.

The Dartmoor National Park Authority protects some of the most breath-taking scenery and nature in Britain, providing free access and facilities for all to enjoy, while balancing the needs of visitors and residents alike. Along with the scenery, the role of the DNPA is also to protect buildings and places of architectural and historic interest. To do that it endeavours to maintain established farming use by encouraging land-owners and managers, as well as local people, to take a part in preserving one of Britain's most special wild and worked landscapes.

Notable people and places

A fact that surprises many visitors is that Dartmoor National Park Authority itself owns very little land. Private landowners

Southern marsh orchids, a feature of wet meadow.

and larger estates, including the Duchy of Cornwall, South West Water, National Trust, Forestry Commission and Ministry of Defence. control the majority. On the moors and in the mires, pastures and reservoirs, woods and plantations, specially designated areas reduce the risk of damage to the environment. In addition, nature reserves such as those managed by the Devon Wildlife Trust help to protect rare and endangered wildlife, ranging from orchids to otters, and butterflies to spawning salmon.

Right: The White Lady Waterfall plunges 30 metres in Lydford Gorge.

Prehistoric remains can be found all over the moor. Even the shortest walk is likely to lead to a substantial relic from the past. Clapper bridges, stone crosses and roundhouses, standing stones, tumuli and cairns all add to the historic significance of the area. New finds continually add to their story and excite archaeologists, including a carving of a cross found in a stone wall by walkers in October 2010, and the remains of a ceremonial site and settlement lying submerged in a reservoir, first revealed in 2009.

Most of Dartmoor National Park lies over a granite plateau around 180 metres above sea level, rising to 621 metres at High Willhays on the north moor. Indeed it is the moor that lures most visitors to its legendary landscape where it is renowned, not least for being the setting for the Sherlock Holmes novel *The Hound of the Baskervilles*. The novel's author, Conan Doyle, based the story on a local tale and, inspired by Dartmoor's remoteness and torrid, changeable winter weather, created a gripping masterpiece.

However, not all the National Park consists of high ground. Some of the most beautiful and surprising places include parts of the surrounding Devon countryside. Rich fertile lands to the north and south of the moor were formed on even older marine sediments and volcanic rocks from the Devonian and Carboniferous ages. Known as Hams, these areas provide a very different landscape to explore.

Farming and tourism are actively encouraged on Dartmoor and go hand in hand: one to help manage the landscape, the other to facilitate its enjoyment. The conservation of ancient farmsteads, villages and towns remains high on the list of priorities, so too does the protection of the moor from the erosion of rural life by stealth. The strict control of light pollution and traffic signs set the moor apart in our increasingly homogenised modern world as a place where people can escape the frantic pace of twenty-first century living. Yet demand for contemporary comforts still allows for modest development in new employment and housing, thereby enabling the local communities to thrive.

National Park attractions

Within the National Park boundary, both English Heritage and the National Trust retain some fascinating historic properties. The English Heritage portfolio includes many prehistoric settlements and ritual stones - Hound Tor, a deserted medieval village and Okehampton Castle. National Trust properties include Finch Foundry, Castle Drogo and the dramatic Lydford Gorge.

Certain sites inevitably attract numerous visitors. The towns of Chagford, Ashburton and Moretonhampstead bustle with activity year round, while Widecombe-in-the-Moor, with its annual fair in September, is undoubtedly the most celebrated. Like many moorland towns and villages it provides an abundance of charm, delicious cream teas and welcoming country pubs. In contrast Princetown has a very different draw. Here, towards the centre of the moor, lies one of Britain's most infamous buildings. Dartmoor Prison attracts thousands of visitors every year to view its rather sinister edifice from afar. So it is not surprising the surrounding community has a thriving tourist trade. Princetown is also home to the National Park's popular High Moorland Visitor Centre, which contains a wealth of innovative displays and lively information. Special exhibitions every year add to the attraction, along with comfortable tea rooms, hotels and hostelries close by. It is said that every town and village within the National Park has a distinctive character waiting to be discovered, and countless people spend many a happy hour sampling scrumptious local food and drink in that quest.

Widecombe-in-the-Moor church is an impressive landmark in this small but famous village.

"Drink real Devon cider and always put cream on your scone first, strawberry jam on top. They do it differently the other side of the Tamar. I wonder how they make sandwiches?"

Combestone
Tor provides
broad views
of open moor,
valley wood
and farmland.

6. Cattle, sheep and ponies
The importance of free-roaming stock herds

Dartmoor owes its appearance and much of its wild nature to the largest animals that roam freely across its uplands. Since people first settled on the moors over 5,000 years ago, their nibbling hordes of stock have kept the ground clear of trees, pruned the scrub and mowed the sward. Cattle like lush grass, while sheep prefer to crop the shortest growth and trim young heather. Ponies browse on a variety of plants including rushes and gorse, a prickly meal that sheep will choose only in hard times. Mixed grazing of cattle, sheep and ponies maintains a variety of rough growth and grasses that in turn create a patchwork landscape rich in wildlife. Although some grazing animals appear to be present year round, more cattle are turned out during the spring and summer months. Over the centuries Dartmoor's four-legged gardeners have been busy chomping on all except the bracken in their path. And despite appearances, all these animals have owners.

Facing page: A classic Dartmoor scene – hill ponies browsing fresh gorse near Haytor.

Hill farmers have a long and humble history. Their life is demanding and even dangerous, tending their animals in some of the most atrocious conditions imaginable. It is no coincidence that cattle, sheep and ponies became the creatures of choice for these farmers as they complement each other in their food preferences. However, the particular breed has great importance. They must be tough and have another important trait - ideally individual herds and flocks should not roam widely across the whole of Dartmoor as it would be a challenge for farmers to find them. It is remarkable to learn, therefore, that some breeds can be trained to graze in just one locality. Nationally the technique is known as hefting, but on Dartmoor it is called 'learing' and the chosen area is called a 'lear', perhaps a local term for an animal's lair. Successful learing may require several flocks or herds to graze adjacent to one another on open, common ground. This way the animals are encouraged by each other to stay in their own space, rather like the pieces of a jigsaw. If a flock is removed from the moor, other animals soon move in to fill the gap, making the most of extra grazing.

The numbers of cattle, sheep and ponies on the moors can vary from season to season, and from year to year. Compared with their population in the early days of the National Park,

right to graze the Commons of Devon, except for some obscure reason the deprived folk of Totnes and Barnstaple. Today, some two-thirds of the moorland is classified as common land, which accounts for just over a third of the entire National Park. The actual process of common grazing is regulated by the Dartmoor Commoners' Council, which has some 850 members, although for various reasons less than half this number now exercise their right - resulting in a greatly reduced livestock presence on the moor.

Cattle

The black or dun and eye-catching Belted Galloway breeds of cattle, distinguished by the white band around their middles, seem to be the most popular hardy breeds on the moor today. Others favourites include a few herds of Welsh Blacks and some Blue Greys. Highland cattle are also to be found on the moor, and tend to attract the most attention from visitors. Despite being one of Britain's oldest, most distinctive and best-known breeds with their long, thick, flowing coats and majestic sweeping horns, they are relative newcomers to Dartmoor.

The South Devon is the traditional gentle giant of the county with rich, medium-red and copper tinted coats; these cattle are most often to be seen roaming during the summer months. The Red Ruby Devon, another local favourite, is now recognised internationally for its ability to produce the very

Black Hereford cattle, ruminating with a view of Hound Tor.

numbers of cattle on the moor today have crashed. Climate, economics and politics have all played their part in regulating the number of Dartmoor's seemingly free-roaming animals. However, tradition has a far more significant role in this demise. Historically, every inhabitant of the county had the finest beef in harsh conditions. These cattle have a great future in farming where they are becoming ever more popular for conservation grazing.

Sheep

Three breeds of sheep can be commonly encountered on the moor. The Scottish Blackface is hardy and adaptable, so it is not surprising that it is one of the most popular breeds in Britain and on Dartmoor. Not only is it the newest arrival here since the nineteenth century, but this breed has now usurped the Welsh Mountain sheep as the predominant flocks on Dartmoor.

The Whiteface Dartmoor is the traditional hill sheep, thought to be one of England's most ancient breeds. Originally these spread across Dartmoor, Devon and west Somerset, but as more land became enclosed from the medieval period up to modern times, the breed has been driven back to its roots. Dartmoor is where the Whiteface sheep still flourishes as one of Devon's premier native breeds. They evolved and thrived on the hills of Dartmoor and here they still graze heather during the summer, moving to hay meadows on lower ground during the winter and spring months.

The Greyface Dartmoor is a so-called 'improved' sheep. Large, long-woolled, attractive, quiet and easily handled, this breed

has its enthusiasts across the country. Descended from the local lowland breeds in and around Dartmoor, the Greyface easily survives the severe winters and exposed conditions upon the open moor.

Whiteface Dartmoor sheep – one of Britain's most ancient breeds.

Not all ponies on Dartmoor are pure-bred. Most are hybrid hill ponies.

The Dartmoor pony

"To ride a horse is to ride the sky." Whoever originally wrote these words must surely have ridden across Dartmoor.

History on the moor

The Dartmoor pony is as much an iconic symbol of the moor as the great granite tors that dominate the skyline. The ancestor of Britain's native ponies first trekked overland from Alaska to arrive here some 130,000 years ago and at the end of the last Ice Age they returned again to roam across the country's extensive grasslands. However, dramatic climate changes that took place around 9,600 years ago started to restrict areas of open grazing as dense wildwood began to cover all but the wet and high ground. Gradually, herds of wild horses became isolated on the moors and mountains of Britain, forming the ancestral stock from which all British hill ponies descend.

The pony is not just a small horse – ponies are actually much stronger than horses. They are renowned for their hardiness, tolerant as they are of a wide range of conditions including extreme cold. Ponies are also famed for their intelligence, sometimes even proving a bit stubborn. Today we define a pony as measuring less than 12.3 hands high. Interestingly, the word 'pony' itself seems to be derived from the old French word *poulenet*, meaning a foal or a young, immature horse, which a pony is most definitely not.

Remnant populations of prehistoric pony, or perhaps a similar breed reintroduced by the Celts, survived on uplands and in remote valleys between 4,000 and 2,000 years ago. Intriguingly, archaeologists excavating on Dartmoor in the 1970s discovered hoof-prints in a Bronze Age settlement, tangible evidence revealing that ponies were perhaps domesticated around that time. Wild ponies grew to become an integral part of everyday life. Tamed and trained, they carried Iron Age hunters, pulled Saxon ploughs, helped shepherd Norman flocks, drove cattle and served as pack animals. In more recent times they were bred to pull traps and small carriages, worked on farms and in mines hauling food and ore. The first written record of the pony on Dartmoor is a reference to the 'wild horses' of Ashburton, owned by the Bishop of Crediton in AD 1012.

However, by the early twentieth century railways and motorised transport relegated their importance and the number of wild ponies dwindled. Although still valued for riding and driving stock, few were used in the commonplace roles they had occupied just a century before. Today, only a small population of wild ponies survive in Britain, and the Dartmoor pony is one of the most famous. In fact, the ponies that we like to imagine as running wild are actually 'semi-wild' or 'semi-feral', rarely if ever handled. The majority are today owned by farmers and dedicated breeders who usually belong to one of Britain's ten official native-breed societies, set up to protect Britain's remaining pony heritage.

Not every pony to be seen on Dartmoor is a true Dartmoor pony. In the past many breeds have been let loose on the moors – everything from pint-sized Shetlands in an attempt to breed suitable pit ponies, to various coloured piebald and

THE DRIFT

The annual Dartmoor Pony Drift is an important social event in the farming calendar. Every autumn the ponies on the moor are rounded up and gathered into nearby pounds. Sorted by owner and the foals weaned, some are selected for sale in local markets at Tavistock and Chagford; the remainder are then returned to the moor. This process provides income for the farmer from wild ponies, and the viability of the practice and continued presence of wild herds is ultimately dependent on the price fetched for the stock each year. No profit, no ponies.

skewbald, also Fell pony, Welsh pony and even an Arab stallion. The latter was actually an attempt to rectify the short legs becoming common among the pony breeds after the introduction of Shetlands among the stock.

Rare breed

The Dartmoor pony is currently listed as a rare breed because fewer than 1,000 breeding mares remain. These days most pure-bred Dartmoor ponies are confined to fields and paddocks to maintain their pedigree, being far too

valuable to let loose. Even the best looking 'native' Dartmoor pony living on the moors these days has often run with mixed breeds, and so it is impossible to prove its parentage.

True Dartmoor ponies can be bay, brown or black in colour. They stand up to 12.2 hands high to their withers at the base of their long, shaggy mane - that's about 1.27 metres or 50 inches tall. Not big by horse standards, but sturdy and strong, they have a small head with large, wide-set eyes, alert ears, and a strong neck, back and hindquarters. A hardy creature that's versatile and a surprisingly good jumper, they live long and have excellent stamina. Above all, the real Dartmoor pony is said to be reliable, gentle and calm with a wonderful flowing gait when seen cantering across the moor.

Dartmoor Pony Moorland Scheme

In 1988 the Dartmoor National Park Authority supported the Duchy of Cornwall and the Dartmoor Pony Society in a new scheme to improve the quality of ponies running on the moor. The aim was to motivate interest among hill farmers to breed a true Dartmoor pony with the natural instinct and attributes of its ancestors to withstand the rigors of their upland home. They set about improving the breed by re-introducing pedigree blood. Approved mares spend the summer running with a registered stallion in one of the 'newtakes', large walled areas in the central moor where the public has access or can view the ponies on a guided walk.

Dartmoor hill
ponies know
how to keep cool
on hot days.

The Dartmoor Pony Heritage Trust also actively supports the aim to revitalise the original breed.

Dartmoor National Park Authority's own grazing herds

In 2003 the National Park Authority introduced a herd to its land on Holne Moor. The project soon expanded into three native Dartmoor pony herds and some mobile grazing herds.

Consisting of neutered non-pedigree males to preserve the blood line, these herds are used as transportable conservation teams; moving from site to site they graze areas of high conservation value just off the moor. The ponies are less discerning diners than cattle or sheep, which is especially important where much of the semi-natural vegetation is rough and poor in nutrients. Grazing by Dartmoor ponies has become vital to ensure the survival of many rare plants and animals.

7. Wildlife
Hawkers, harriers and hippos

Spring arrives late on the moors, often a week or two behind the rest of Devon. Walking is easier at this time of the year, as long as you avoid the boggy bits. Picking your way between the winter-browned heather and low-growing western gorse is simpler and safer if you follow the nibbled grass tracks. Heading into the valley beyond Haytor, a fan of converging paths leads down to an old gate encrusted with lichen, framed between rough granite posts. Summer is not far away, the air is warm, and a carpet of bluebells beckons.

Right: A golden-ringed dragonfly rests on rosebay willowherb.

Facing page: A bellowing red deer stag, most commonly found on the western moor.

Here, the call of curlew fills the morning air, rising and falling like the surrounding hills. Some curlew have not travelled far to breed on the moor, having spent the winter months on the southwest coasts probing estuary mud flats for food. Other birds travel much further and a faint but distinctive cry announces their arrival. The cuckoo conveniently calls its own name, which is perhaps just as well because few people ever see one. Large, low-flying and rather hawk-like, the cuckoo lands on a wall and calls its name once again. Wintering in Africa south of the Sahara, the birds return here in late spring. Once a familiar sound in the Devon countryside, cuckoos have become sadly rare outside the National Park. Dartmoor is still good meadow pipit territory - ideal potential foster parents for a baby cuckoo.

THE TALE OF A MAN AND A MOTH

A previously unknown species of moth discovered in an ancient Dartmoor wood was named after a solicitor who took early retirement to pursue his passion for insects. Initially the finding was thought to be a colony of moths that had blown in from the continent. However, DNA tests and examination by a leading Dutch scientist, a world expert on micro-moths, confirmed the species was new to science.

Ectoedemia heckfordi, or the Heckford pygmy moth, was officially named in April 2010 for amateur naturalist Bob Heckford from Plymouth, surely the ultimate accolade for any entomologist. The miniature moth is only the second new species of its kind to be discovered in the British Isles in the past 50 years. And it was found in a small patch of National Trust woodland on the banks of the River Dart.

The new moth may only be 6mm long but it is the first completely new species Bob Heckford has ever discovered, and this was by pure chance. Driving home to Plymouth, Bob decided to stop and take a rest. While examining the leaves of a nearby oak sapling, he spotted the tiny green caterpillar of a 'leaf mining' moth.

He said: "I knew straight away it was something new to the British Isles because all the larvae of the ones that live on oak leaves here are either white or colourless, and this was a bright emerald green." He has since found other examples of the same previously unknown species in Hembury Woods within the National Park, but none elsewhere – so far.

Dartmoor National Park is much more than high windswept uplands and treacherous bogs. From limestone caves to peaty streams, fern-filled woods and farmland, the wildlife within its borders is a very special mix. Being the largest and highest upland in southern Britain it is not surprising that the nature here is exceptional. Areas of international importance cover more than a quarter of the area, including blanket bog, moorland heath and remnants of ancient oak wood.

Dartmoor is a stronghold for scarce butterflies; in addition several rare breeding birds and bats do spectacularly well here. Out of the 17 species of bats known in Britain, Dartmoor sees 15 species, including the very rare Barbastelle and Bechstein's bats. Even more remarkable is that Dartmoor can claim a flower and a moth found nowhere else in the world – the Vigur's eyebright, rediscovered in the late 1990s, is found only in the far south-west of England, and the Heckford pygmy moth appears unique to the National Park.

Apart from these real rarities, what is it that makes Dartmoor's wildlife so special? Some spots are certainly very rich while others can appear poor, mainly because of the severe weather conditions on the high moor. But it is this elevation that contributes to making Dartmoor utterly unique in southern Britain. The difference in temperature between Devon's coasts and the top of the moor can be several degrees, making winters here longer and summers shorter. So Dartmoor is

Nightjar feeding two fluffy chicks – demonstrating their incredible camouflage.

Northern wildlife

Two evergreen shrubs that thrive in the cool climate of uplands and Arctic tundra can be found on Dartmoor. Crowberry, with its heather-shaped leaves, produces pale pink, drooping flowers and has edible bright red fruit. It is mainly confined to a few scattered patches in the northern blanket bogs of the high moor. In contrast, cowberry has shiny, dark green leaves that are more box or cotoneaster in character, and bright red berries. Cowberry is limited to just a couple of patches on the southern moor near Holne.

The most notable breeding birds include golden plover, dunlin and red grouse. But they are sadly now few in number and mainly confined to the north moor.

Southern wildlife

Some mainly Mediterranean species reach the northern limit of their range on the milder fringes of the moor. The ivy-leaved bellflower has tiny pale blue blooms and the bright yellow marsh St John's wort is common in shallow-flowing streams.

In 1995 a colony of the rare southern damselfly was discovered on Dartmoor. Restricted elsewhere to a scattering of locations in North Africa and Western Europe, its British strongholds include the New Forest and Pembrokeshire. In Devon the only colony previously known is in the east of the county, over 25 miles away from Dartmoor.

Two enthralling southern species of birds have also made Dartmoor their home. The nightjar is a migrant that winters in Africa and returns here each summer. An extraordinary, enigmatic creature, its cryptic colouring, large eyes and huge gaping beak give a clue to its lifestyle. Being nocturnal, this intriguing bird feeds on moths and other night-flying insects, and relies on incredible camouflage to brood its eggs on open ground.

The Dartford warbler is resident only in the southernmost reaches of the UK, living here year-round. A small, dark, long-tailed warbler, it may perch on top of a gorse stem to sing, but is more often glimpsed as only a small flying shape bobbing between bushes. Widespread in the warmer parts of continental Europe, feeding on spiders and small insects, the Dartford warbler is vulnerable to population crashes during severe winters and loss of breeding areas as a result of gorse fires.

manage their land for the benefit of wildlife for all to enjoy, and many wild plants and animals have indeed benefited from various conservation initiatives in recent years. The nature of Dartmoor's wet places can broadly be divided into Rhôs pasture, wet woodland, valley mire and blanket bog. The latter two are the realms of carnivorous creatures and predatory plants, the home of dragonflies and damselflies.

Blanket bog

Rare elsewhere in the world and confined mainly to sub-Arctic regions in Britain, Dartmoor's blanket bog is one of the most southerly to be found anywhere on Earth. Blanket bog forms in the highest, wettest places. Remote and bleak, the flora and fauna of bog may be scarce, but is far from boring.

On Dartmoor a combination of impervious granite and high rainfall creates the ideal conditions for sphagnum moss to grow, and 12 different types can be found here. Sphagnum mosses are extraordinary primitive little plants, capable of carrying many times their own weight in water. After centuries of growth and decay in the acidic, water-logged conditions, layers of this dead plant material can build up to more than half a metre thick. Topped by patches of new moss, this wet ground is also home to purple moor grass and the fluffy white seedheads of common cotton grass, as well as splashes of the yellow blooms of bog asphodel. Other plants frequently found in blanket bog include deer grass,

A young toad in a valley mire has the ability to change colour, but there are limits.

an island outpost for plants and animals from much further north, yet around the moorland fringes they also encounter life from the warmer south.

The beauty of bog and other wetlands

Work to restore important areas of Dartmoor's blanket bog continues apace in collaboration with South West Water and conservation organisations. The National Park Authority also provides advice to farmers and landowners on how best to

wetlands. In recent years declining numbers have reduced the breeding success of these attractive little waders to a mere handful of sites.

Valley mire

Dartmoor is internationally important for the mires, the stretches of boggy ground that form in valleys situated around 300 metres above sea level. They often occur in basins, and sometimes in the so-called newtakes, which are the large

Left: Common cotton grass is often seen on blanket bog and valley mires in midsummer.

hare's-tail cotton grass, round-leaved sundew, cross-leaved heath and, sometimes, crowberry.

Small insects such as aquatic flies do well in this environment in summer, and they attract keeled skimmer and black darter dragonflies to feed. The fly larvae also provide a rich source of food for some bog nesting birds. Golden plover and dunlin are at the southern edge of their northern range, so have never been abundant breeders on Dartmoor's high

SPHAGNUM MOSS

This extraordinary moss has the sponge-like ability to absorb and hold water. Growing in clumps with no roots, 12 different species of sphagnum are known on Dartmoor, ranging from bright green to red in colour. Each varies in their ability to colonise new areas and each flourishes in slightly different conditions.

The plant has been much used by people over thousands of years for its absorbent and cleansing properties – uses that range from toilet paper to baby's nappies. During the First World War the moss was collected on Dartmoor and sent to the Western Front as dressings for wounds.

summer droughts. Rich in wild plant and animal life, swathes of cotton grass, and colourful patches of cross-leaved heath, bog asphodel and bog bean, flourish here. Carnivorous plants thrive in the most nutrient-poor ground, gaining nourishment from other sources - in the Dartmoor mires three species of sundews and the pale butterwort lure insects to a sticky end before absorbing their body fluids. Other plants common to these mires include marsh St John's wort, moorland water crowfoot, bog pimpernel, several sedges and bog mosses. For the botanical buff the fir club moss is a great find, and an equally rare delight is the sight of a bog orchid or some Irish lady's tresses.

Huge golden-ringed and black darter dragonflies patrol these wetlands in summer, both snatching smaller insects from the air. Keeled skimmer dragonfly and the endangered southern damselfly are less likely to be encountered, but still seem to be surviving well in scattered locations.

Remarkably, common frogs spawn on Dartmoor in the depths of midwinter, their gelatinous masses of black eggs protected by a layer of ice, sometimes for weeks on end. Toads can also be seen in the lower valleys; sometimes they attempt to take on the colour of the surrounding vegetation, although pink bog pimpernel will always prove a bit of a challenge. Grass snakes hunt the mires for tadpoles, frogs and palmate newts. And in the heat of midsummer adders

A damselfly is ensnared by the sticky tentacles of a carnivorous sundew.

walled areas found in the central part of the moor as well as around the edge. Most of these lands were taken from the former hunting lands of the ancient Dartmoor forest by the Duchy of Cornwall during the late 1700s and early 1800s. Some valley mires on Dartmoor are also associated with the old tin streaming works that effectively dammed valleys, thereby allowing peat to accumulate.

More sheltered and often deeper than blanket bog, many mires retain their moisture even during the most severe

DARTMOOR'S WILD HIGHLIGHTS

- The harsh 'cronk' of a passing raven or the plaintive mew of a buzzard overhead.
- Ancient oak woodland and wild daffodils beyond Steps Bridge at Dunsford.
- Skylarks pouring out their liquid song from a clear blue sky.
- Blanket bogs on the high north moor where dunlin and golden plover nest.
- The magnificent hay meadows near Postbridge.
- Small heath and fritillary butterflies on the moorland fringes near Belstone.
- Traditional farmland, drystone walls and hedgerows rich in wild flowers around Widecombe-in-the-Moor.
- Carpets of spring bluebells near Kennick Reservoir and Holwell lawn.
- Marsh and other orchids in valley mires at Drizzle-combe.
- Hobby chasing a dragonfly in August at Burrator Reservoir.
- Heathland ablaze with colourful western gorse and heathers at Haytor.

Far left: The hobby is a fast-flying small falcon that spends the winter in Africa.

Left: Western gorse and heather colour rocky tors in July.

A young roe deer is left alone while its mother feeds in Rhôs pasture.

retreat to the Dartmoor valley mires, sunning themselves on dry islands of heather and grass.

Curlew and lapwing are sadly much less common today, but the snipe is still breeding regularly in the valley wetlands, particularly on the eastern side of the moor. Their drumming display flight is a real treat to hear, the strange sound emanating from stiff little tail feathers held out as the snipe dives through the air.

Rhôs pasture

In some places the valley mires blend into grassy wetlands away from the open moor. Known as Rhôs pasture - a Welsh term - these grazing lands rich in species support a variety of grasses and rushes, usually enclosed within farm walls. In the National Park, Rhôs pasture is commonly found near streams and small rivers where ponies keep the vegetation under control during the summer months. Dartmoor contains some of the biggest and best areas of this rare pasture type that is seldom found outside Britain.

This wet grassland contains several interesting and distinctive plants, including marsh plume thistle, devil's-bit scabious, heath spotted orchid, saw-wort, sharp-flowered rush, creeping willow, ivy-leaved bellflower and large expanses of purple moor grass. Some special butterflies also live here -

the attractive marbled white and small pearl-bordered fritillary, and the beautiful marsh fritillary, which has now re-occupied many sites on Dartmoor, improved conservation management succeeding in nearly doubling its presence since 2005. The birds most commonly encountered on these wet meadows can include snipe, reed bunting (another potential foster parent of the cuckoo), grasshopper warbler, woodcock, barn owl and short-eared owl. And the wild mammals most likely to be seen by day will most likely be the fox and roe deer.

Wet woodland

Ancient oak wood and open parkland form the greatest tree cover in the National Park, but in many places the ground is so waterlogged that only a few types of tree can tolerate such conditions to thrive. Grey and goat willow along with alder sometimes border streams, and groves of low-growing willow thrive in and around the valley mires; here downy birch and ash can also be found. The attractive flowering marsh marigold, opposite-leaved golden saxifrage, marsh violet and great tussock sedge compete with fountains of vivid green ferns and bog mosses. A rich and diverse lichen community and the occasional regal fronds of a royal fern add to the botanical importance of these wet woodlands. The bird life is also fascinating, attracting redpoll, siskin, willow tit, and woodcock with its wonderfully long beak.

Marsh marigolds in April – among the earliest flowers to be found in wet woods and by streams.

Cold water

Numerous small streams drain the high ground of Dartmoor and feed 18 main rivers - most head to the south coast, while just a few head north. Cold, clear streams and dark peaty rivers rise and fall with the seasons. They trickle seductively on a summer's day and at other times flow in full spate with their banks brimming, barely containing the raging torrent. Along these tumbling and gurgling moorland streams and faster flowing rivers, the aptly named dipper and grey wagtail both do what their names imply. Active little birds, they seldom stand still - the dipper dives underwater to feed on

Mink and otter are both widespread on rivers in the south-west of England and both live along the watercourses of the moors. Dartmoor has always been a stronghold for the native otter, yet it is the least likely of the two to be seen, as otters tend to be highly nocturnal; mink will hunt all hours. Devon has the dubious distinction of being one of the first places in Britain where mink successfully went feral. Introduced to Britain in 1929, these animals escaped from fur farms adjacent to the River Teign in the 1950s. Luck was on their side - the fact that five of the region's major rivers spring little distance from each other probably gave this troublesome little hunter access to all parts of the county in a fairly short time.

Dartmoor has always been a stronghold of the otter.

tiny aquatic larvae, while the wagtail takes what insect life it can find from the surface.

Salmon and sea trout migrate from the ocean to spawn in many of Dartmoor's main rivers. While the adult fish feed on little or nothing during their journey, the young spend up to two years feasting on freshwater invertebrate life. On Dartmoor they compete with the resident trout, grayling and the smaller, more nocturnal loach and bullhead. Although trout and salmon do feed on emerging mayflies, it is the mid-water drifting hoards of tiny creatures that have either lost their footing or get dislodged that form the bulk of the food for these fish.

The high rainfall feeds plenty of man-made leats, temporary pools and farm ponds where aquatic insects and amphibians can thrive. So it is not surprising that when people started looking for water supplies on a larger scale they constructed eight reservoirs on Dartmoor. As no natural lakes exist on the moor, reservoirs now provide the only large expanses of open water for wildlife. Water birds make the most use of these places, and herring gull, cormorant, Canada geese, pochard and tufted duck are all regular visitors. But perhaps the most interesting is the goosander, a spectacular bird that spends the day diving for small fish on fast flowing rivers. In winter small parties of goosander gather on the reservoirs, and occasionally larger groups of over 40 birds or more have been counted.

Dry moor

Grass, bracken, gorse and heather dominate different areas of dry open moor, but grass moor offers even less opportunity for wildlife than the heathland, which often supports only a limited number of plant species. Late summer is a glorious time for colour on the open moor because this is when ling, bell heather, cross-leaved heath and western gorse are all in bloom. Where bracken and gorse grow few other plants can compete, but in the patches between the taller vegetation small flowers often grow in great numbers. Getting down on your hands and knees is the best way to appreciate the beauty of tiny tormentil, milkwort and even smaller heath bedstraw flowers.

Surprisingly, flower-filled heather moor is not the richest place for insect life, but insects that can survive the harsh conditions often thrive here because of little competition. The fox moth is probably the most commonly seen large insect of its kind and its silky-haired, fawn-coloured caterpillars can be conspicuous on grassy tussocks between July and September. The Emperor moth is larger and even more spectacularly marked, although less common. Emperor caterpillars are large, strikingly marked in bright green with black hoops, and can be found hidden among the heather during summer. The adult moth emerges during April and May, and can sometimes be seen flying fast and low over the

Above: July to September is the best time to see ling or common heather in flower.

Left: The emperor moth is Britain's only silk moth, emerging in late spring and early summer.

The marbled white butterfly thrives on traditional farm meadows around the moor.

keep to drier slopes while the large blue butterflies favour similar sunny areas with close-cropped turf and patches of wild thyme. Once declared extinct and although still rare, they have been re-introduced to secret locations on Dartmoor.

Of all our butterflies, the large blue leads one of the most bizarre lifestyles, providing a real challenge for conservationists. Their caterpillars feed on wild thyme then rely on a particular species of red ant to carry them deep inside their underground nest. The little caterpillars pretend to be baby red ants, secreting chemicals and making noises to fool the ants. Once inside the ant nest the caterpillar feeds on the ants' eggs and young for several weeks, before pupating. When the butterfly finally emerges the following summer, the ants even escort the butterfly safely to the surface, guarding it until its wings are dry.

Other butterflies lead less complex lives. During the summer months near bracken or woodland, large silver-washed, high brown and pearl-bordered fritillary butterflies may be most conspicuous, feeding from wild flowers. Smaller purple and brown hairstreak butterflies are restricted to where they can find food plants for their caterpillars in the form of young blackthorn and oak leaves. In contrast the beautiful little green hairstreak butterfly is much more widespread, especially where whortleberries flourish.

heather top. The only other moth to be found on the moor is the small and delicate-looking plume moth, most frequently found among the bracken.

Meadow brown butterflies commonly live in the same habitats as gatekeeper, small heath and marbled white butterflies, and their caterpillars all feed on grasses. Common blue and small copper butterflies tend to be locally common, which means they can be few and far between, but where you find them they are often in strong numbers. Grayling butterflies

Beetles are common on the moor but are less often seen as most keep close to the ground. The exception is the common tiger beetle with its spectacular green colour and rose spots. These active little hunters can be seen scurrying around and flying over the heather in early summer, hunting for other insects to consume. The handsome northern bumblebee is the only wild bee commonly active on the high moor throughout the warmest months. The domestic honeybee can sometimes be seen, but only a handful of today's bee keepers maintain the old tradition of bringing hives to the heather. On fine summer days many damselfly and dragonfly can be encountered, especially on the dry fringes of valley mires. Elsewhere - not just around blanket bogs and open pools - stronger, faster-flying dragonflies, such as the golden-ringed variety can be seen in midsummer, sometimes far from any wetland.

Common lizards can be found anywhere on dry, open moors, especially on sunny, south-facing slopes along walls. And wherever lizards are common so too will be the venom-ous predator that feeds on them - the adder. This is not a creature to be handled and must be treated with the utmost respect. Adders are well camouflaged, shy and sensitive to disturbance; consequently moorland adders are seldom noticed. Only on cool, sunny days and early in the morning can they sometimes be slow to move.

Wheeling high above, or perched atop, a granite tor, the buzzard is one of most common birds of prey on the dry moor; the other is the hovering kestrel. Much rarer is the sight of two smaller falcons, the tiny merlin perhaps chasing a skylark, or the glimpse of a fast-flying hobby falcon swooping after a dragonfly. Sightings of a Montagu's harrier are occa-sionally reported, but short-eared owls and hen harriers are more common. They hunt most years across grassy plains

Britain's only venomous snake, the adder is common on Dartmoor although seldom encountered.

The endangered woodlark survives on farmland in the steeply wooded Teign valley.

also be seen flying between bushes, and up and down to the ground, wherever gorse and bracken dominates.

Above an altitude of some 400 metres, always take a second look at blackbirds. While these common birds may occasionally be found here, so too can the rare ring ouzel, distinguished by its characteristic white bib. A summer visitor, the ring ouzel is occasionally seen near quarries and abandoned buildings but its favourite place is among old tin workings, especially where mounds of mining spoil have created a chaotic, cratered landscape of miniature gorges and mountains. On the moorland fringes, such as in the Teign valley, farmed fields and nearby woodland, the rare woodlark can also sometimes be found, singing its melodious song.

Apart from domestic stock, the rabbit must rank among the most common mammals on the moor. Dartmoor was one of the earliest places where rabbits were introduced to Britain, as food in the twelfth century. Place names that contain the word 'warren' are a reminder of the economic importance of this mammal in the past.

The Dartmoor fox is said to be paler than its lowland relatives. But this is probably because, with fewer trees, they spend more time in the open and the sunlight subsequently bleaches their coat. Lowland foxes feed extensively on earthworms; however, in the acid, calcium-deficient soils of

and heather moor, particularly in spring and autumn, sometimes even in winter. The raven can be heard at any time of the year, their distinctive 'cronk' call being the easiest way to distinguish them from a passing rook or crow.

Birds bring the moors to life in summer. This is when the song of skylark and meadow pipit pour down from the blue skies. On the high tops a few nesting red grouse, dunlin and even golden plover may still be found, but they tend to keep largely to inaccessible bogs. Dartmoor is the English stronghold of the wheatear. Usually seen among granite clitter and alongside stone walls, its flashing white rump is an easy way to identify this striking bird. Stonechat and whinchat can the moor worms are absent and snails rare, leaving only the rather unappetising black slugs. So moorland foxes feed mainly on short-tailed field voles and rabbits, both of which are widespread on the dry moor. Foxes are mainly opportunist scavengers, taking any carrion they find - despite plenty of anecdotal evidence to the contrary, they do not kill sheep or take healthy lambs. Stoat prey on rabbits and weasel hunt for smaller mammals, principally wood mice and voles. The tiny common shrew searches for insects deep inside heather and tussocks of rough grass, and only children or those with exceptional hearing will hear its high-pitched, even ultrasonic, shrieks.

High tops

Blasted by gales and drenched in rain, frozen for much of the winter and baked dry in summer, the high tops of the granite tors are tough places for life at any time of the year. Only in the deepest cracks can plant life endure the extreme weather conditions, so here stonecrop and lichen, as well as tiny liverworts, mosses and ferns, cling to a precarious existence. Lower down, black spleenwort and a few stunted whortleberries and heather plants grow between bare, broken boulders. Ponies, cattle and sheep often seek shelter in the lee of rocky tors and their nibbling limits the plant growth found here. But it is the very top of the tor that provides the best vantage point on a clear day, something that both birds and people alike have enjoyed for millennia.

Stonecrop and rock-hugging lichen flourish in the extremes of the high tops.

Oak woods and plantations

The vast majority of Dartmoor's native woodland grows on some of its steepest, rockiest slopes, just as it has for perhaps three thousand years or more. Little disturbed, the natural processes of timber death and decay produce a profusion of fungi and an army of leaf-living creatures from mites to millipedes. All the British species of slug can be found here, and many wood-boring beetle larvae are food for battalions of foraging birds in this habitat.

Legendary trees

After the last Ice Age, when freezing Arctic winds had given way to a warmer temperate climate, a vast forest covered most of lowland Britain - across much of England this wild-wood was dominated by great oak trees. Over time people gradually cleared the land and only in the most isolated parts did remnants of that original woodland survive. High on Dartmoor some vestiges of that oak wood still cling to a few hillsides today. Remote and spooky places in the half-light or swirling mist, the gnarled and twisted trunks of these trees are draped with thick growths of moss, lichens and ferns - no wonder they spawned so many sinister stories in the past.

Three ancient patches of wood are officially recognised on Dartmoor: Black Tor Beare, Piles Copse and the weird, wonderful and most well-known Wistman's Wood. The woodlands consist mainly of the common pedunculate oak along with some rowan, also known as mountain ash. Although they do grow close to their maximum altitude, what makes the trees found here so remarkable is their strange and stunted stature. Today, few trees grow on the high moor apart from conifer plantations, isolated hawthorns and rowan; perhaps the most incredible fact about Dartmoor's relic oak woods is that they survive at all.

Valley woodland

Huge valleys slice deep into the edge of the moor, and large, deciduous woodlands cover many of the valley slopes, spanning rivers and hiding streams. The woodland edge is generally richer in wildlife than deeper inside. Damp and dreary in winter, the depths of woodland are cool and shady in summer. Some areas of this deep woodland are so inaccessible they provide a glimpse of what the woods may have looked like in prehistoric times - an impenetrable tangle of fallen trunks and rotting branches. Some native oak woods within the National Park are so significant they have been assigned special status. On the eastern edge of the moor is a wood first mentioned around the mid 1500s, in an inventory of King Henry VIII's forests; today, Yarner Wood is an important part of a National Nature Reserve. Here enormous wood ant nests rise from the woodland floor and spectacular pied flycatchers and redstart regularly breed.

Ferns flourish in the damp atmosphere of these valley woodlands, sometimes even growing on the trees. And they are not alone. Whortleberry can be found sprouting high above your head; even more amazing is the sight of a rowan tree growing from an oak. Down on the woodland floor ivy, honeysuckle and sometimes sallow thrive between the rocks, and where the soil is deeper a luxuriant growth of larger ferns can carpet the ground.

Dark plantations

On first sight, densely planted conifer forests can appear unfriendly for wildlife. But where felling operations create clearings these plantations can also be home to some rather interesting birds. Crossbill, nightjar and lesser redpoll, not

Facing page: The greater butterfly orchid does well only in old hay meadows.

otherwise commonly found on the moor, all breed in and around these sites. Although conifers make up the bulk of the plantation, their edges are sometimes softened by beech and other deciduous trees. This adds to the wildlife value of these ephemeral forests, grown to harvest in decades.

But perhaps one of the greatest benefits of plantations for wildlife is not within but beyond the woods. Conifers provide good protection against wind; so where these trees encircle moorland reservoirs the shelter they provide attracts many fragile insects and small birds that otherwise might not survive here. And there is one rare bird that almost exclusively frequents conifer forests, one that is sure to get even non-birders in a flutter. The powerful, low-flying goshawk is impressive, with a wingspan almost as big as a buzzard. A small number of these wary predators have now made Dartmoor their home, preying on medium-sized birds from wood pigeons to carrion crows.

Farmland

Small fields enclosed by granite walls, hedges bursting above stone-faced banks of earth and sturdy thatched farmsteads fringe the National Park. It is the character and richness of the farmland that adds immeasurably to the distinctive character and beauty of Dartmoor. Here the soil is often less acid, more fertile, and deeper. Traditional, less-intensive farming has allowed flower-rich hay meadows to survive along with

ancient boundaries, hedgerows that still link woodlands and scattered areas of scrub. The result is a picturesque landscape rich in wildlife, where orchids grace the meadows and butterflies rise in your wake. Dormice survive here, as do tiny harvest mice, both becoming relatively scarce elsewhere.

The late cutting of hay allows meadow flowers to set seed, important for annual hay rattle and late flowering devil's-bit scabious. A rare fern, moonwort, also grows in some meadows and butterflies abound in many more - ringlet, meadow brown, gatekeeper, marbled white, small heath, small copper and common blue butterflies are all common on the farms at the edge of the moorland. Six species of bumblebee take advantage of these wild flower meadows, including the upland-loving mountain and the heath bumblebees.

Arable fields around the moorland margin are a less common sight, growing wheat, brassica or maize. Apart from some arable weeds the wildlife of these fields is scant, but they still provide valuable foraging areas for many farmland birds - linnet, skylark, yellow hammer, meadow pipit, chaffinch and even the nationally scarce cirl bunting are to be found foraging here in the winter months. When rabbits are scarce on the ground, buzzards will feed on mice, beetles and crane fly larvae, as well as huge quantities of earthworms. They will even follow tractors when ploughing.

Dartmoor's underworld

If you need an antidote to the wide open, windy expanses of the moor, head for Buckfastleigh. Here an extraordinary secret world was discovered when Victorian workmen were quarrying for marble and uncovered a labyrinth of caves. Created by rivers and streams as they followed natural fractures and fissures in the rock, a series of passageways and cave chambers had been dissolved and eroded over vast periods of time. Water continued to furnish the voids, seeping through cracks in the limestone and forming droplets that hung from the roof deep underground. As carbon dioxide dissolved in the water it was released into the blackness of the cave atmosphere, leaving a tiny ring of calcite around the water drop. Eventually the drip fell to the cavern floor and was replaced by another on the ceiling, the process being repeated as the millennia passed so that slowly these calcite deposits grew.

The best cave formations occur when the climate is warm and plant growth outside on the surface is producing sufficient carbon dioxide to dissolve the limestone - during the cold Ice Ages calcite formation was therefore slow. Eventually, however, great stalactites hung from the roof and stalagmites grew to meet them from the floor; crystal pools also developed where lime-saturated water was trapped in small basins. Sometimes even more weird and wonderful

The colours of cave formations can also be spectacular. While pure calcite is white, staining from other dissolved minerals in the water can produce dramatic streaks and washes of unearthly hues: iron stains red, copper stains green and manganese stains black. Generally the entire process is painfully slow - depending on the cave, it can take over a thousand years for a calcite formation to grow just a couple of centimetres. However, not all caves take millions of years to form; where miners once dug for tin and copper around the fringes of the moor, abandoned mines have created many other new caverns for wildlife to exploit.

Beyond the threshold of light, the inside of a cave is a world of utter darkness. Here beneath Buckfastleigh only the sound of dripping water breaks the silence and the temperature remains remarkably constant, around 12°C all year. Near the cave entrance a strange luminous moss can be found which reflects the faintest light to produce a subtle green glow. Further inside sun loving plants can no longer survive; even the most shade tolerant ferns and mosses struggle deeper within, until they too give way to bare rock.

Yet even the blackest holes can support a variety of life. To survive here, creatures need only a limited ability to detect light, and with skin colour serving no useful purpose, permanent cave dwelling animals tend to be devoid of pigment and virtually blind. Some cave pools support tiny

Left: The rare greater horseshoe bat is a social creature, but roosts together in very few places.

formations occurred - where fluctuating water levels periodically flooded a cave and then receded, barely discernible drafts of air created fantastic irregular shapes known as helictites. Depending on the conditions and rate of dripping, the result can produce a simple distorted cone, a curtain, or even the shape of a little man.

HIPPO IN THE DART

Before the last Ice Age the wildlife of Devon was very different – during this previous interglacial period creatures such as hippo wallowed where the River Dart now flows. Nearby lion hunted herds of elephant and hyena caught their own prey or scavenged from kills. The collapse of a cave roof on a hillside over 80,000 years ago opened up an entrance to a new den, a place where predators could hide and devour their meals. Over time, the chamber gradually filled with mud and bones until finally sealed by the rising mound of debris, thereby creating a natural tomb.

In 1939 some enthusiastic young cavers began exploring tunnels previously exposed by workmen at Higher Kiln Quarry. Over ensuing seasons the pile of mud and bone, known as a Talus mound, was partially excavated. Today these remarkable remains form the richest collection of mammal bones ever discovered in a British cave. They include the tooth of a baby elephant along with the bones of rhino, wolf, bison, hippo and giant deer, still lying where they were buried, now barely a stone's throw from a busy dual carriageway.

communities of freshwater shrimps and lively little copepod relations. In the twilight zone nearer the entrance, pink and white woodlice forage the floor along with small beetles and even smaller springtails. More impressive, the cave spider is the only British species to be found living exclusively in mines, holes and caverns. These spiders weave a silken sac suspended from the ceiling to hold their eggs and hatchlings.

The onset of autumn brings in new life from the growing cold. In summer caves are cool, yet in midwinter they can be relatively warm, allowing small tortoiseshell and peacock butterflies to survive the winter months underground. But the most spectacular insect to hibernate in caverns is the herald moth, hanging in a state of suspended animation from damp cave walls.

Other creatures seem to prefer a crowd. Bats are the largest cave dwellers to spend the entire winter in the dark in hibernation, not so much a tactic to survive the cold as a strategy to prevent starvation, as between October and April little or no insect food is available for bats to hunt. While eight species of British bat inhabit caves, only two can be found together in large numbers. Both the lesser and greater horseshoe bats live at Buckfastleigh caves, with up to 500 individuals sharing a single roost.

8. Dartmoor people

Dartmoor today is a product of its people, both past and present. Its moorland the result of thousands of years of hill grazing, its structures and buildings a tribute to the talents and determination of generations of farmers, miners and craftspeople. Indeed, few landscapes preserve such abundant evidence of prehistoric and medieval lives. Yet the creation of the National Park in 1951 helped transform Dartmoor from a forbidding, often inaccessible upland to one renowned for its scenic beauty, vibrant tourism and innovative local businesses.

While the setting is special, it is people that make the National Park what it is today. The following is a selection of those who currently live and work on Dartmoor – some involved in its management, a few famous and others well known in their local communities. All share a passion for Britain's most iconic national park.

Bill Hitchins
Chairman, Dartmoor National Park Authority

Bill Hitchins began his working life as an agricultural nutritionist, and used to visit farmers all over the south-west, including its moors. "It was a wonderful opportunity for me to discover Dartmoor, finding farmsteads tucked away in some of the most remote locations, sometimes miles from the nearest road. For 25 years I travelled all over Dartmoor, always fascinated by its people and absorbed by its history." But then Bill has a distinct advantage when it comes to seeing the National Park from a wider perspective.

Living on the edge of the moor and owning a smallholding qualified him as a commoner with rights on Roborough Down. He also served as Treasurer to the Roborough Commoners' Association for 30 years. Bill joined Bickleigh Parish Council in 1983 and took the Chair a little later. A few years after that he was elected as a South Hams Councillor, where he has held the posts of Deputy Leader and Chair of Council, the portfolio holder for prosperity, historic environment

champion and the nominated representative to the National Park. So it was no surprise, with a background in local government such as his, dealing with issues as varied as clay mining, upland grazing and military training, that he was appointed as Chair of the Dartmoor National Park Authority in 2009. Bill followed a long line of distinguished people who have held this important post, from landowners to a retired naval officer. "My role," he explained, "is to support the Chief Executive and build the skills and representation of the Authority members. I am now even more involved with the moorland community and like to have an open door policy to my office. In fact," he laughed, "I don't have a door to my room, so it's always open."

His involvement in youth recreation and sports provision also gives Bill a young person's point of view. And his district council responsibilities allow him to indulge a personal interest in fortresses because 42 Commando is based in his ward. "However, I have recently seen a very different side to service life, meeting families of the war casualties. Dartmoor's tranquillity is a great healer. Its peace and quiet helps if you have lost someone close," he said seriously. Bill then revealed

A buzzard's eye view of the northern moor provides a rare perspective.

that one of his favourite places to visit is the western moor, especially around Burrator. "Taking a flask of coffee, it is a great place to sit and enjoy the surroundings. I even read some of the papers I need for meetings up there. It is not just the detail that counts, it's so important to look at the broader issues relating to the National Park." And it is here that Bill

has a real advantage. His son was trained as a pilot and now flies helicopters commercially, often providing his father with a bird's eye view. Seeing the aftermath of a large fire at Fernworthy or a remote archaeological site from the air enables Bill to see a much bigger picture of Dartmoor National Park than most people.

Dr Kevin Bishop
Chief Executive, Dartmoor National Park Authority

A colleague at the Countryside Council for Wales first drew Kevin Bishop's attention to the advertised post at Dartmoor National Park. As a keen walker and mountain biker, with a background in countryside planning and protection, Kevin was no stranger to Dartmoor. Born in the West Country, he originally set out on an academic path in geography and land management. Since then his personal and professional fascination with national parks has taken him across the length, breadth and heights of Britain, from Scotland's coastal paths to the mountain peaks of Wales. Becoming a member of the World Commission for Protected Areas means he has also indulged his love of wild places on a global scale. Yet Dartmoor was always a favourite for family holidays.

When appointed Chief Executive in 2007, his first challenge was to get to know and understand Dartmoor's people and places even better, as he revealed: "This is my dream job, but I also realise that I have to turn that dream into a reality. My aim is to ensure that the Authority helps to maintain the National Park as a living landscape where people and nature exist in harmony, and where there is a positive relationship between landscape and livelihood." Kevin was heartened by the warmth of welcome he received from so many people. "The Authority staff and members, Dartmoor residents and visitors all have a wonderful passion for the place," he remarked. He was also intrigued by the changing seasons. "Following the winter snow, when the moors seemed almost as busy as midsummer, the coming of spring is marked by swaling. It is like a ceremonial burning as the farming community celebrates the end of the coldest months," he observed.

There have also been some unexpected encounters, and one was particularly memorable. Travelling from Holne to Princetown one sunny morning in his early days on Dartmoor, he was delayed by some cattle on the road. Stopping the car he turned off the engine and opened the window to talk to the farmer watching his dogs and helpers herd the animals along. A 'thanks for waiting' turned into a longer conversation as the cattle slowly made up their minds where they wanted to go. Seizing the opportunity of a friendly ear to have a morning grumble, the farmer poured out his woes - the sorry state of national hill farming and problems with a planning application. Then he suddenly stopped and looked worried. "Do you work for the National Park . . . you're not a planner?" he asked hastily, looking relieved when Kevin said that he was not a planner. "So what do you do?" he asked. When Kevin finally had a chance to introduce himself, he was not sure which of them was more embarrassed. "But the farmer's face was a picture," he smiled.

Then, when Kevin's eldest son took part in his first Ten Tors Challenge, he was truly inspired both as a father and head of the National Park. "There is no comparable event anywhere else; while the level of organisation was impressive I was not prepared for the spectacle. It was like a scene from the film *Zulu* as thousands of excited youngsters swarmed across the hillside at the start. Then half an hour later they had all vanished from sight."

Kevin's empathy and enthusiasm for Dartmoor is very evident but he is still realistic about the challenges it faces. Dartmoor is obviously a special place, unique among national parks for so many reasons, not least for the fact that over its 60-year history it has seen only three Chief Executives, and all still reside within the National Park. That alone speaks volumes about its character, its people and its purpose.

Part of a school team strides out at the start of the annual Ten Tors Challenge.

Dr Nick Atkinson
Chief Executive (1991–2007), Dartmoor National Park Authority

Many people dream of finding a job that might have been made just for them. For Nick Atkinson it was more luck than intention. When his favourite newspaper went on strike he bought another that carried an advert for the position of a forester with Dartmoor National Park Authority. His background in forestry and recreation land use seemed ideal - and it was. "Dartmoor is special," he remarked. "Where in this crowded country can you be alone on the highest hill in midsummer on a Sunday afternoon and where else is the night sky so dark in England? If only there was wider recognition that our native oak woodlands are every part the match of tropical rainforest." Nick Atkinson is as passionate about trees as he is about Dartmoor. Not surprising, really, he spent more than 33 years with DNPA, first as Senior Forestry Officer, then Head Ranger and Deputy Officer, before finally becoming its Chief Executive for 16 years. Nick retired in 2007 with many happy memories, and a few embarrassing incidents he would rather forget.

Just before arriving to take up his new post with the National Park Authority he visited Meldon near Okehampton. "It was no doubt the reservoir that attracted my wife and I to visit the place, innocent of the battleground the valley had once been. I know how desolate I would have felt if another such battle had been waged and lost while I was at helm. Standing above Meldon, the scene before us was witness to four great dramas, historic flashpoints that marked the evolution of the National Park - army training, a vast quarry, a reservoir and a dual carriageway. Each was a desperate intrusion, masking the loss of important archaeological and ecological detail that characterises Dartmoor. Yet the grandeur and splendour of the moor transcends these intrusions, which is not to excuse the developments but to recognise that awe is a rare emotion. Dartmoor demands spiritual, practical and moral respect in return."

Of all the posts Nick held on Dartmoor, one must stand out. His explanation was typically self-effacing: "I've enjoyed every job I had on Dartmoor. For me it was the right time in the right place. But my best time was undoubtedly as a ranger. Everyone loves a ranger," he grinned beguilingly. "But there were some occasions, like the hippy invasion of New Bridge, which were not pleasant," he scowled. Other times were almost farcical. Driving up to Haytor one morning a cigarette packet came flying through his open window from a passing car. "I eventually caught up with the offending vehicle at Widecombe and did my 'ranger' bit, politely quoting the local bye-law concerning litter," explained Nick. "The offender turned out to be what I thought was a lady until I heard her language. The stream of abuse and swearing was uncalled for. So next I did my 'policeman' bit, from a friendly warning it was now pending prosecution and so started to take her name and address. At that moment her husband leapt from the car and approached me. But far from being threatening he was so apologetic, explaining that this is what he had to put up with all the time! I felt so sorry for him I let them off with a warning."

Diplomacy and the meeting and greeting of visiting dignitaries from home and abroad are all part of the role of Chief Executive. But it is not always easy to make the best impression no matter how hard you try. Haytor is a favourite location to bring visitors for spectacular scenery. "After one official reception," remembered Nick, "I took a small party up to the top car park at Haytor. An immaculately dressed French lady stood out from the rest, wearing a designer dress and very high heels. Not the best wear for the moors - added to which she spoke no English and the view was hidden by thick fog!"

The breathtaking view of Haytor from Rippon Tor is well worth the climb.

Professor Ian Mercer, CBE
First National Park Officer (1973-1991), Dartmoor National Park Authority

When Ian Mercer first visited Dartmoor as a geography student in the early 1950s, little did he realise how much the place would feature later in his life. The landscape both fascinated and puzzled him. Intrigued by the granite piles of Combestone and Bench Tors on Holne Moor, he began to wonder why many of the near-vertical fractures looked as if they had been prised apart. Expanding ice could exert enough force to do this, but rainwater would simply drain away before it could freeze. Only on a field trip to the Canadian Arctic did he solve the dilemma. During the Ice Ages, snow packed the cracks hard and it was this snow that froze, not the rain. Ian's eyes light up when he talks about landscape.

In 1959 he was appointed by the Field Studies Council to set up a new centre and nature reserve on the South Devon coast at Slapton Ley. Dartmoor became his favourite location to explain his passion for landscape to legions of keen young students. It was the climax of the geography course but not of Ian's career. As the County Conservation Officer for Devon in 1971 he expanded his horizons and responsibilities. Dartmoor National Park was run by a Committee of Devon County Council until 1974 but from then on it became an Authority, directly accountable for its funding and future. Ian became the first National Park Officer to be appointed in Britain. "A bit daunting," he said with a smile, "but, without any precedent, at least I could make it up as I went along."

The offices for the new National Park were first, as he described, "just sheds at the back of County Hall in Exeter." A presence closer to the National Park became a priority. The opportunity to move to a National Trust property near Bovey Tracey was exciting. "For the first time we felt like a National Park Authority." However, the real work was just beginning: everyone seemed to have their own version of a management plan and establishing agreements between the Authority, landowners and farmers took up much of his time.

Some negotiations had very satisfying outcomes and he remembers one well. It concerned a Duchy tenant farmer who was struggling to work his land alone. Grazing was difficult to control without fencing but the Authority preferred to maintain the old granite-style walls. So agreement was reached to pay for a full-time worker, and the farmer's son came back to the family land. "That," added Ian, "was when I learnt that curves are quicker to build than corners, and it's why newtake walls have so many bends."

Apparently the virtue of such a compact national park as Dartmoor, some 20 miles by 20 miles, is that it is popular with visitors from overseas, especially official ones. On one occasion Ian remembers standing on Haytor with the Minister responsible for national parks in Turkey. The Minister asked Ian if the rangers had any special powers. "They have a warrant to enforce bye-laws and to help advise the public, what about yours?" The Minister said that in Turkey his rangers had the power to shoot to kill. Seeing Ian's surprise, he explained that they were bedevilled with tree poachers. Timber trees are rare and valuable in Turkey, and the poachers were armed. It made Dartmoor seem thankfully tame by comparison.

In 1991 Ian resigned from DNPA to become Chief Executive of the Countryside Council for Wales and then Secretary General of the Association of National Park Authorities. He is the author of many books, including the prestigious *Dartmoor* in the Collins New Naturalist series, published in 2009. Today, he still lives within the National Park's boundaries and plays

Combestone Tor reveals textbook granite jointing and erosion.

a major part in its life as Chair of the Dartmoor Commoners' Council. "After a lifetime of landscape, I think it, live it and love it," he said. No doubt he always will.

103

Dru Butterfield

Dartmoor Pony Heritage Trust

"One of my earliest childhood memories", observed Dru Butterfield, "was the drum roll of the cattle grid as our car passed into the National Park. Even to this day the vibration of the wheels crossing the grids sends a shiver of excitement up my spine. It may seem ridiculous to some that a person can be so moved by a place, but this is what Dartmoor does to me and why I feel so motivated to protect, educate and inform visitors to its many wonders. In 1951 Dartmoor National Park was gifted to the people of this country. I can think of no better present to our nation, a place that inspires and provides respite. In these challenging and pressured times, every man, woman and child deserves the right to space - and what precious room Dartmoor gives us."

Dru is also passionate about Dartmoor ponies. Not so much the modern, multicoloured, crossbred kind, but the original ancient pony that has roamed Dartmoor for thousands of years. Indeed, so enthusiastic is Dru about maintaining a viable population of these rare creatures that she helped found the Dartmoor Pony Heritage Trust. Now assisted by some 30 eager volunteers, their new centre is based close to the headquarters of Dartmoor National Park Authority, near Bovey Tracey. The Trust does great work with many children, whether partially sighted or educationally disenchanted, and they learn as much about themselves as the ponies. Apart from educating people about the true Dartmoor pony, the Trust also aims to preserve these animals by adding value to foals. As Dru explained: "A feral, untrained foal for riding may fetch £50 on a good day at auction, and if sold for meat, far less. But a ready-trained, easy-to-handle pony is worth more than twice as much. That makes the Dartmoor pony more of an asset to hill farmers, ensuring the pony's future." It is a clever tactic.

Watching Dru training a newly weaned foal - barely six months old and fresh from the moor, wide-eyed, uncertain and edgy - was an education. The work is highly skilled, brave and physically demanding. Dru's calmness and careful approach reassures the young pony that it is in safe hands. A soft rope is gently draped around the foal's neck. Slowly

Dru takes up the slack, avoiding eye contact. The foal resists, digging in its little hooves and leaning back on its haunches. But as soon as it relaxes, Dru releases the rope. The principle here is pressure and release - and in just a few minutes the foal learns not to resist. Next a halter is offered. The foal sniffs and tastes it before the halter is quietly slipped over its head and the stroking begins, with a glove on a stick so Dru is less likely to get kicked. Gently rubbing her extended hand along its mane, neck, withers and front leg, along its back, tummy and rump, then down its rear leg, reassures the foal. First one side gets the treatment, then the other. After ten minutes the foal is led to another pen to relax, eat and drink.

Six foals in all started the process of halter training that morning. Some have been easy to work with, others more challenging. Occasionally a feisty foal 'explodes', then there is more work to do. Around three hours training for each foal over the next three days will enable the ponies to be safely caught, led and transported, checked by its handler and even have its hooves trimmed without stress or injury.

Dru's technique with the foals has been honed over years of practice; it is undoubtedly strenuous yet impressive to watch. Dru maintains it is not horse whispering, purely hard work. It just looks like magic.

Dru maintains that there is no mystery to her work – it just looks like it.

Richard Drysdale
Sustainable Development Officer, Dartmoor National Park Authority

For someone who once cycled from Japan to Australia via China, Vietnam and the islands of Indonesia, pedalling across Dartmoor must seem relatively straight-forward. Today, Richard's daily commute takes him across Trendlebere Down with far-reaching views over Lustleigh Cleave and the Wray valley. He casually mentioned, "It's downhill most of the way to work but uphill on the way back." He believes it must be one of the best commutes in the world, and positively glows while talking about the beautiful dawns and vivid sunsets, as well as the early morning mists lying in the valley below.

However, on moving to Dartmoor he was not prepared for the utter darkness. The first time he rode home after leaving work when the evenings had started to draw in, he ended up pushing his bike because the headlight was not powerful enough for him to see the road ahead. Now, apart from a new lamp, he has a much more enjoyable journey than his previous commute, negotiating the rush hour traffic from West Hampstead to central London. Indeed, he was so used to busy city roads that he initially found the narrow winding lanes here somewhat daunting. It took just a matter of weeks to adjust. These days Richard is happy to explore even the smallest of side roads by bike. The moorland air and magnificent views set him up for the day and unwind him before he gets home. "Dartmoor energises, relaxes and inspires me," he said with sparkling eyes.

Richard's previous career was as a manager in the responsible travel industry. Married with young children, the family did not need to leave London but wanted to raise their children in a better environment. Offered a post at Dartmoor National Park Authority in 2007, Richard jumped at the chance and is now completely immersed in village life. "Everyone here is so friendly. It was not long before I found myself helping with a variety of things in my local parish. And as our children grow up they now see the world in a very different way."

He continued to explain: "Dartmoor people have always had to be more sustainable than most. It's the only way to survive

Dartmoor offers plenty of adventure – including kayaking in autumn and winter for these youngsters from a local college.

on the moors." Richard's role in the National Park Authority is to promote sustainable tourism, adventure activities and transport across Dartmoor, as well as to manage the funding applications for sustainable development awards. This involves liaising with a wide range of people, both within the Authority and across the National Park. The awards help to support everything from renewable energy and local events to farm diversification, community schemes and enterprise projects. He added, "I am so lucky to meet so many people and work alongside colleagues who all have such a pride and passion for the place."

Is he taking life any easier after moving from the big city to the moor? I think not. Although work is busier than ever, Richard's idea of fun is to take part in the annual Dartmoor Classic, a 105-mile gruelling challenge for even the most experienced cyclist. Just the thought probably leaves most people breathless.

Geoff Hearnden
Farmer, conservationist and
Chairman of the Dartmoor Sustainable Development Fund

The beautiful Teign valley with its sparkling river, banks of wild spring flowers and shady glades seems a world away from the heights of the surrounding hills. Nearly 300 metres above the valley floor, travelling up a steep winding lane, a Dartmoor tor suddenly appears from nowhere, peeping from beyond a high hedge and granite stone wall. Passing some impressively restored medieval thatched barns the track eventually ends at the home of Geoff Hearnden, a more modern-looking farm but one with equally ancient origins. The sound of squabbling sparrows, chattering swallows and a host of other small birds fills the morning air. "This place looked a bit different when we first found it in 1960. It had been empty for a couple of years and we approached it through a tunnel of blackthorn."

A first generation farmer who originally trained at the nearby Seale Hayne Agricultural College, Geoff and his wife Janet bought their farm and 30 cows soon after setting eyes on the place. Geoff vividly remembered his early days on Dartmoor. "Three years of restoring a derelict farm and milking the cows twice a day was followed by the disastrous long winter of 1963. The situation called for a major rethink. We needed to set up a system which might produce adequate returns in the future and so we sold the cows and went into pigs. We fancied a farming system not entirely dependent on subsidies. Many other changes have happened since then, for instance two once-busy blacksmith's shops nearby are now transformed into a holiday let and a pub. A real sign of the times. Concern for conservation hardly existed when we first started farming here; so much energy was put into ploughing and draining ancient grassland."

Even as a boy Geoff had a passion for wildlife, nurtured by an inspiring schoolmaster. Owning a farm has allowed him to indulge himself, not only in nature but in history too. He taught himself to read the landscape, noticing hedge lines and field shapes, and discovered archaeology on his land spanning more than three thousand years. Even a dry patch

Far left: A spindle whorl and flint scraper from over 3,000 years ago, and an oxen shoe and clay pipes from the early 1800s.

Left: Nesting swallows mark the start of summer on a Dartmoor farm in May.

in the garden lawn turned out to be the remains of a sixteenth-century house. Here Geoff uncovered a fireplace between two large, blackened stones and found plaster, pottery and clay pipes. However, his favourite pieces are a stone spindle whorl and many flint flakes and scrapers all left by prehistoric people, who also farmed this land. His children took some of these finds to school and this led to archaeologists from Exeter University walking the fields in search of more artefacts.

Geoff became involved with the Devon Wildlife Trust in his early years on the farm, first volunteering for conservation work, then as a trustee and chairman. Today three generations live on the farm; the pigs are long gone and wetter land is planted with trees or is being restored to flower-rich pasture by spreading hay from the moor's few remaining ancient meadows. "Dartmoor is our home and our grandchildren share it with us. Living in a national park is a great privilege and joy for us all," said Geoff. Still active on the board of the Devon Wildlife Trust, a long-serving parish councillor and Chairman of the Dartmoor Sustainable Development Fund, he has long been a supporter of the aims of the National Park. He is modest about his knowledge of wildlife, but if asked, can tell you the exact day that swallows and other migrant birds have returned to the farm over the past few decades.

John Weir
Head of External Affairs, Dartmoor National Park Authority

It helps to be passionate about places to be a good geographer, and for John Weir the two are inextricably bound. Born in North Staffordshire and immersed in the Peak District landscape and culture from a young age, his love for glaciated uplands eventually led him to the heights of Snowdonia. From there, Dartmoor beckoned as a landscape affected but not sculpted by moving ice sheets.

John first came to Devon in 1974, as a student at Seale Hayne Agricultural College. In his personal quest to discover what lay over the horizon, he explored moorland villages and walked the hills. "That initial fascination with Dartmoor has always stayed with me. One of my first impressions was the beautiful scenic relationship in Chagford, between Endecott House, the Church and distant views. Another was being followed by a ring ouzel down Steeperton Gorge. I was particularly drawn to the high tors of the north moor and the distinctive whale-back outline of Cosdon."

John joined the National Park Authority as Information Officer a short time later and one of his first tasks was to organise the library. "Unfortunately, my preliminary field-work was cut short by a broken ankle, so I was confined to the office for several weeks. Very frustrating for someone who enjoys the open air so much."

The National Park Authority has come a long way since its early days, and John has been closely involved in its development over the last 30 years. The move of staff from Exeter to Bovey Tracey brought the Authority closer to moorland people. The building of the Okehampton bypass caused high emotions, as did the foot-and-mouth disease outbreak in 2001, as John revealed: "Despite the disaster and resulting impact on everyone's lives, I felt very privileged to work for the benefit of the National Park throughout that crisis. Although stressful, at least we could help, and it brought us closer to the Dartmoor community."

Today, John's National Park Authority role is wide and involves many aspects of Dartmoor life, including information, lifelong learning, media relations, publications, museums and exhibitions, to name just a few. Obviously proud of what it has achieved, he continued: "The National Park Authority has accomplished so much; without it people's experience would be much the poorer. We have a hand in so many things - from facilitating the rebuilding of stone walls to grazing and public access, the latter being defined two decades ahead of national regulations. The Dartmoor Commons Act 1985 was one of the most important achievements of the Authority. It took 11 years to come to fruition and two goes through Parliament. We even helped find a solution for public access to Finch Foundry, when it looked as though its future was in doubt. Working in partnership has been, and remains, key."

John's knowledge of the moor and its people is impressive. "The West Dart is a particularly favourite area of mine, especially watching trout rising and the sun setting over the moor. Just getting to Fur Tor is a journey in itself. Easdon Tor is another outstanding location; so is St Lawrence Chapel and Whiddon Deer Park. But perhaps just being there is more important than any particular place. I don't have so much a favourite place, just memorable experiences. Each one is different but none is any the less."

Finally, one experience John will never forget. "For me Dartmoor is a Pandora's box of delights. I particularly remember watching a group of London children, from Wandsworth, on their first Dartmoor tour. They had never before run in an open landscape. They could go wherever they wanted. It was amazing to see and they really enjoyed themselves." John relived the moment with a big smile, a picture of someone who loves Dartmoor and every aspect of its life, and what it can bring to people.

The dark, peaty waters of the West Dart flow beneath Wistman's Wood.

111

Robert Steemson
Head Ranger, Dartmoor National Park Authority

To become a National Park Ranger was always Robert Steemson's ambition, even as a young boy. He was not put off when his teacher asked, "A warden on Dartmoor, is that a career?" But he did have some inside knowledge. "My mother was born from generations involved in farming on Dartmoor. And although my father was in the RAF, he fell in love with Dartmoor and my mother while on leave." Robert was born and brought up on the moor and went to Widecombe-in-the-Moor School. His weekend playground was the river and rocks around Spitchwick. Now he is a Governor at his first childhood school.

The life of a ranger can be demanding and dangerous, especially when rescuing walkers and stranded motorists from snowdrifts, floods or moorland fires. Today millions of people visit Dartmoor. So liaising with landowners and moorland communities, managing the car parks and leading guided walks, repairing paths, collecting litter and cleaning up after road accidents is all in a day's work for a ranger such as Robert. When the vastness of the moor is your workplace, and the tasks sometimes seem insurmountable, the peace and pleasure of the landscape still make the work endlessly rewarding. The Head Ranger has the added responsibility for organising his team, assisting them in enforcing the bye-laws and ensuring their safety. "Managing volunteers, dealing with the owners of problem dogs and helping visitors is more about education than enforcement," added Robert tactfully.

Since becoming a ranger Robert's role has never stood still. In his early days the moor was always quiet in winter, especially when the snow lay deep. Now four-wheel drive vehicles and snow ploughs keep the main routes clear, and popular slopes remain accessible for families to enjoy sledging and throwing snowballs. Dartmoor is busy all year round with people horse riding, canoeing, climbing, rambling and running; others come simply to enjoy peace and solitude. One of Robert's most hectic periods is the lead up to the Ten Tors Challenge, a major event itself. This annual Challenge has tried and tested generations of teenagers from across the region and the rest of Britain. Hundreds of schools and colleges, along with thousands of participants, need the army to organise them for the event. Coordination with the military, farmers, team leaders and the emergency services requires Robert's constant attention.

It was on such a day in 2008 that Robert introduced the new Chief Executive of the National Park Authority to some of the Ten Tors organisers. They saw the event start and met the military over breakfast at Okehampton camp, before proceeding to another meeting in Fernworthy Forest. Robert squirmed in his chair at this point: "It was all rather embarrassing," he admitted. "With my boss in the car for the first time, I got the four-wheel-drive stuck in the mud. I even had to get some soldiers to haul us out. Very humiliating. And if that was not bad enough, my boss thought the entire episode so funny he shared a giant photograph he shot of the scene with all the staff at the Christmas party. I never lived it down!" He roared with laughter at the memory.

A good sense of humour obviously helps to handle the demands of being on the front line in the National Park. If proof of Robert's credentials in public relations were ever needed, his talent to take on a variety of roles, from the Dame to Simple Simon, in the village pantomime at Leusdon every Christmas must surely help.

The vantage point and scenic beauty of Haytor makes this a popular place for visitors and a busy location for National Park Rangers.

Angela Rippon, OBE

Broadcaster and journalist

"No matter where in the world I am, Dartmoor is never far from my thoughts," beamed Angela enthusiastically. "I have a very public job, watched by millions of people worldwide, so the opportunity for real solitude on the wild open moors is something I love and treasure. I never cease to be amazed that one moment I can be in the bustle of New York's Times Square, yet in less than 24 hours I can be enjoying the peace and quiet of Dartmoor. Devon is my real home." Born and brought up in Plymouth, Angela's Royal Marine father was a keen cyclist and at weekends they often explored the South Hams, Edgecombe and Dartmoor by bike, as well as travelling further afield by car. "As a child, Dartmoor was my playground. I have wonderful memories of swimming in cold moorland rivers at Hexworthy and Cadover Bridge."

Angela Rippon has been a familiar face and voice in British broadcasting for more than four decades. Trained as a journalist in her hometown of Plymouth with the *Sunday Independent*, she then worked for both BBC Plymouth and ITV Westward Television, before joining the BBC National News team in 1973. The first female journalist newsreader, Angela danced her way into the hearts of the British public by making two memorable appearances in the *Morecambe and Wise* Christmas shows. Her award-winning career has since spanned an impressive diversity of radio and television programmes in Britain, Australia and North America.

Away from the media limelight Angela is an accomplished equestrian. Her first horse was called Katie, as she recalls: "She made it possible for us to cover huge distances across Dartmoor. I would happily ride for three hours, reaching parts of the moor that I could never have walked to. Up so high with views over Plymouth to Cornwall, Katie gave me a real sense of freedom." Dartmoor also means much more to Angela than just somewhere to escape - it is a source of inspiration. As the author of a veritable library of books, from bestselling biographies to keep fit guides, it was the successful children's stories featuring Victoria Plum to which Dartmoor contributed most, as Angela pointed out: "In

Walkham valley the stone walls with entangled roots gave rise to the idea of a 'fairy tenement', a block of flats inhabited by slow-worms and spiders, wrens and wood mice. The stories were based on actual seasons and real wild creatures."

These days, after travelling back from the USA, Angela revels in the anticipation of returning to her parents' old home on the edge of Dartmoor. "I love coming home to Devon, the 180-degree views of Dartmoor from the house change dramatically with the seasons. One day there is mist, the next clear. Whether covered in snow, a storm brewing, or clouds rolling in the sky with their shadows chasing across the moor, Dartmoor is so beautiful. When I'm home Dartmoor makes me smile. It's the colours, the sunsets and big skies. Even Wyoming can't compare," laughed Angela.

"Dartmoor has given me so many happy family memories, I never feel alone on the moors. The National Park is important not just for me but for the nation, especially as we become more urbanised, surrounded by people living in cities. Young people especially need the opportunity to explore wild open places. It is such a precious thing. My father used to walk for six hours at a time; what could be better than keeping fit in beautiful surroundings? Dartmoor is distinct, different in character to anywhere else with its wonderful tors and craggy skylines. Nowhere in the UK has anything like it. And it's my home," added Angela, again with her distinctive smile.

A favourite with Angela, Tavistock market on the western edge of Dartmoor is a colourful destination for residents and visitors.

Lt Col Tony Clark, OBE
Commandant, Dartmoor Training Area

From Dartmoor to Dartmoor via the World is how Colonel Tony Clark unassumingly describes his life and distinguished military career. Now based at Okehampton Camp, he has spent an impressive 57 years in uniform - from cadet to Colonel. Okehampton was where he was brought up from the age of four, his father a Royal Fusilier stationed at the Camp. And it was to Dartmoor that he returned after the Duke of York's Royal Military School, the Royal Military Academy Sandhurst and service with the Parachute Regiment. An expert in simulation for army training, Tony has managed the exercises of a remarkable number of troops on Dartmoor for over 17 years. His talent for effectively engaging both civilian and military personnel has won him respect and popularity with the local community and much further afield. A flair for making regulations memorable means that pilots flying helicopters into his base for the first time remember the rules. "Easy really," he says shrewdly, "rather than giving them a list, I remind them that the

ponies, cattle and sheep are armed with automatic rifles with a range of 500 metres. And riders on horseback have ground to air missiles, which can bring down a helicopter half a mile away. The air crew don't forget!"

Military training on Dartmoor has its critics, but the majority accept that troops need the best training and that the Armed Forces were here long before the area became a national park. For more than 200 years, from Waterloo to Kandahar, Dartmoor has challenged and prepared many of Britain's fighting forces for war and peacetime tasks. Today, the impact is lighter than in the past and the public are only excluded during live firing for their own safety. In his own inimitable words Tony explained. "Dartmoor provides troops with holidays with a purpose. And with 130,000 bed nights a year this is the biggest holiday camp in the south-west," he grinned. "Not that Dartmoor is a holiday for the soldiers. The landscape here is sharp, not rounded by glaciers. And bad weather is an asset. Survive on Dartmoor and you can survive anywhere in the world. My role is to advise, assist and supervise." The Dartmoor training area is unique in Britain, the only one where everything must be cleared up after each military exercise. A staff of 11 help with the clearing up, often finding more public litter than that discarded by troops. Horses are used in preference to quad bikes. "For good reason," said Tony. "It is easier to look for items when you are not worried where your feet are going, and horses are more environmentally friendly. Even better, if the mist comes down you just drop the reins and say 'go home'."

Tony has great respect for the moor in work and play, and owns a small farm within the National Park. "Understanding nature helps the military to fight and survive. Local people and wildlife are a vital part of the training process," he added. So too is his role in the annual Ten Tors Challenge for young people and the Jubilee Challenge for less able youngsters, he explained. "The military is proud to support these events and we help participants understand national park purposes, as well as giving them a sense of personal pride and achievement. The Ten Tors is tough whichever distance you choose but the Jubilee Challenge is deeply humbling. I broke my leg a few years ago and so took the chance to borrow a cross-country mobility scooter, to experience what some of the less able youngsters face on the moor. It was real eye opener," he said, full of admiration for all those who take part. "Hopefully I can pass on my fascination for Dartmoor, its ancient remains and the feel of the place. Peace and nature are in my soul, Dartmoor gives me the quiet and space for contemplation."

The exciting start of the Ten Tors Challenge for 2,400 youngsters facing an arduous trek of up to 55 miles.

117

Ron Barter
Master cider-maker

Known locally as 'Devil's brew' or 'rocket fuel', traditional Devon cider is made using age-old methods and is still considered by some to be a magic art. The pressing of apple pulp through straw allows the juice to naturally ferment with wild yeasts from the air and apple skins, but the origin of the process has long been long in the Dartmoor mist. The cider press Ron Barter uses to make Brimblecombe's cider at Farrants Farm in Dunsford is over 350 years old, giving a wonderful sense of how long cider has been made here. This is perhaps the world's oldest cider press still in use; and if that is not impressive enough, there is another, even older apple press in a nearby barn that is no longer working.

Ron is helped by his wife, Beverley, and son, Daniel. Although they have been producing traditional Devon cider here for less than a couple of decades, they believe cider has been produced on the farm for over 500 years. The current cider-making barn oozes age, perhaps even dating back to Saxon

Right: A mountain of cider apples from the Teign valley.

times in origin. A heavy wooden door with handmade hinges creaked on opening as we visited the barn; it was dark inside. Large, low timbers supported a planked floor above before opening up to reveal the great wooden and iron structure of the press itself. Below, the liquid was channelled away in a massive granite trough. To one side fresh straw bales were piled high. The scene was lit by a single light bulb hanging above, heavily draped in cobwebs; a motorised apple pulper seemed to be the only other concession to modern times.

Ron lives, breathes and drinks his own cider. "A good cider has to have a bite," he grinned, taking another sip. "And it has

Above left and right: Layers of apple pulp and straw form the rectangular 'cheese' ready for pressing.

Above left and right: Squeezing the last drop from the apple pulp, Ron keeps up the pressure for hours. The cider will take many months to mature.

to be slightly acidic. When you taste it, it must have character and above all be thirst-quenching. That's why it's a very popular drink."

Outside, a mountain of apples from the surrounding orchards and elsewhere in the National Park glistened with Dartmoor dew. Inside, the subdued sound of friendly chatter filled the dusty air. An eager band of volunteers waited expectantly for the master cider-maker to appear - Ron strode in suitably dressed. Shovels and hands at the ready, the roar and clatter of the apple-pulping machine started somewhere above us, soon followed by the rumble of apples into a hopper. This signalled the arrival of the first pulp slopping down a wooden sluice. From here the mangled apple was delivered on to a straw bed by the shovel load. Ron deftly moulded the mush into a rectangle before calling for more straw. The 'cheeses' of this giant apple sandwich steadily grew layer upon layer.

Everyone worked furiously, taking it in turns to relieve each other of the heaviest work. Just the weight of fruit alone started a steady trickle of juice long before the first cranking of cogs. Then the shoulder-high stack was ready for pressing. High in the loft above, Beverley and Daniel began the laborious hand winding to lower the heavy wooden plate of one of the oldest working presses in Britain. Finally, Ron leant on a long wooden lever to squeeze the last drop. It seemed that every straw fibre was now dripping the sweet nectar that drained into a large vat. Nothing is added. Natural yeasts work their magic converting sugars into alcohol.

The master of ceremonies tasted the fresh juice approvingly, while all around weary bodies collapsed on the remaining straw, exhausted from hours of frantic activity. In the adjoining room, rows of great wooden barrels lined the walls and a heady scent of cider filled the gloom. For our freshly squeezed juice, six months of fermenting lay ahead. It would then be ready to drink, but may be matured in oak barrels for up to six years to suit different tastes. Ron conjured up some cups and soon aching muscles were forgotten, as they must have been for centuries, revived by the awesome power of Devon scrumpy.

FARMERS' FUEL

 Farmhouse cider has a fabled reputation for its alcohol strength and life-giving levels of sustenance. For centuries it was the staple diet of many Devonians, and Dartmoor dwellers were no exception. The orchards of the Teign valley once ranked among the finest and most productive in Britain. At one time virtually every farm around the fringes of Dartmoor and its lower-lying valleys had their own orchard. Some of the crop was cherished for its summer eaters, others as autumn and winter cookers. But the most famous and plentiful apples such as Hand-me-Downs, Slack-me-Girdle, Sweet Alfords and Tremletts were best when brewed. Safer than water, packed with essential nutrients, cider was once the fuel that kept the farming and labouring forces of rural Britain happy at work.

Robin Armstrong

Artist and fisherman

Wildlife and freshwater fish painted with passion from hours of observation is the mark of Robin's distinctive style. His eye for detail and talent for applying colour in both watercolour and acrylic paints come with a sureness of touch that only a real understanding of the subject can produce.

Robin has painted for as long as he can remember, selling his first work at the age of 12 years old to a milkman. He truly discovered he could paint when he found he could not stop painting. His sketchbook diaries are an assorted collection of leather bound albums, picked up for a few pounds from local auctions. Filled with more than just words, they capture fabulous memories of the many locations in which he has lived, worked and played across the globe - many of the sketches found in them form the basis for his larger works of art. He is also the author of six books.

Originally, Robin started work in advertising for the well-known *Fishing* magazine, based in London, but yearned for a less conventional life. Renowned wildlife author Ewan Clarkson facilitated Robin's eventual flight from Fleet Street to South Devon in the early 1970s. One year later Robin and his family discovered the Powdermills near Postbridge, and here they lived for several seasons in blissful isolation. "Dartmoor was a dream come true," explained Robin, "and I was living it in a vast open space. It was a leap of faith and a rather hand-to-mouth existence, but I loved it. And I met so many characters on the moors - other artists, fishermen and even a wildlife film-maker," he grinned broadly at me.

"Painting was always a vocation, not a job, but I needed some real work that would combine my love of fish and Dartmoor. That is how I became a water bailiff patrolling the Rivers Tavy, Walkham and Plym. In those days salmon was really expensive - there was none of this farmed stuff - and poaching could be very lucrative." Robin looked serious for a moment. "The work was mainly enforcement, patrolling overnight and in the small hours, and dangerous. One professional gang operated out of Bridport in Dorset - they even came armed," said Robin, looking alarmed as he remembered a scary night. "I did it to protect the fish and got to know the best pools, every run and where the fish laid up at midday. But after several years the job changed to being a bucket carrier, checking pollution run-off from farms. I met some farmers though who had never travelled far from the moor, not even Exeter!" he said, surprised.

Robin has fished in many countries from Alaska to Australia, but still reckons Dartmoor isn't really the best location for trout and salmon. "At least it is safe here, with no dangerous animals. I don't want to 'go' like an artist friend, killed by a grizzly bear while fishing." But for Robin, the real joy of fly fishing is watching the wildlife. "Egrets and otters have to be my favourite creatures to watch, egrets for their exotic looks and otters for their playfulness. One evening I even had an otter grab a trout I was playing. So I dropped my rod and watched him eat my fish."

His days as a water bailiff were obviously exciting but friends still contact him when they have a dilemma: "One friend asked me to look at some strange damage done to a few trees on his land. He reckoned otters were to blame but when I saw the pencil-sharpened trunks of the young trees, I guessed the culprit must have been an escaped beaver. Whatever

next?" Perhaps they will appear in a future painting, gloriously captured along with the colour of reflections and trailing bubbles. No matter what the subject, Dartmoor will always be his home, his love and his real inspiration.

Rich in wildlife, Dartmoor rivers provide endless inspiration for a talented artist.

Seth Lakeman
Folk singer and songwriter

Described as a dark, brooding presence, this rising star is making English folk music fashionable again and exporting it to the world. Inspired by the myths and legends of Dartmoor where he lives and regularly runs, his songs feature the tragic and romantic tales of Dartmoor's most desolate hills. A prestigious music prize nomination in 2005 for a song telling the sad story of a servant girl brought him wider public adulation as he delivers his foot-stomping, almost hypnotic, yet undeniably thrilling, sound.

A bundle of energy, Seth seemed happy and relaxed to talk for a moment about the place that so inspires him. He came to Dartmoor at the age of just six months, born to parents who were brought together by their shared love of music and who soon successfully established themselves on the southwest folk scene. By the time Seth was nine years old, and with two brothers, the family was writing songs and playing at a nearby pub. "It was a great training ground, music is in our blood," explained Seth. "And my interest in history, especially military history, was inspired by my granddad - he was at the D-Day landings," he said, with obvious admiration.

After working in a band with his brothers for several years, Seth decided to strike out alone with his exciting style of narrative story-song. In 2002, his first album, entitled *The Punch Bowl*, was experimental and self-financed. It showed real promise, but it was its successor, the darker *Kitty Jay*, recorded in his kitchen for £300 in just three weeks, that released his true potential. To his amazement, the album was nominated for the prestigious Mercury Prize, and Seth's solo career took off.

Dartmoor is his inspiration. He enjoys running on the moor and around Burrator Reservoir, not just to keep fit but also to stimulate his mind and absorb the atmosphere. He went on to describe how he plays music in his mind. "It's the rhythm of the run, the scenery and wildlife. All adds perspective to the vision I have for the next song. It can be addictive though," he briefly smiled. "Music is all I know how to do, and now I am enjoying the business side of it too."

And what a business he is developing. Touring, live shows and another album being recorded at Morwelham Quay. He had just returned from Glastonbury, and was playing at the Eden Project over the weekend, when I caught up with him. "Great audience," he commented on Glastonbury. But then his fans always appreciate the energy and skill he puts into his music. He continued, "It's important when you work with your hobby, to keep in love with it. I have taken my songs of Dartmoor around the world and explain each story to the audience, so they become more involved."

The tragic tale of Kitty Jay has moved many of his fans to make a pilgrimage to the moor. "When I drive pass Jay's Grave on the parish boundary, I often see young people who have come to that special spot just to listen again to my song." He looked surprised but should not, such is his gift for engaging the packed houses and outdoor concerts where he plays. "My music today is like Dartmoor - a rugged, mystical sound. Folk music is communication by, and for, people," he explained. But he need not have; Seth Lakeman has a rare, emotion-stirring talent for bringing some of Dartmoor's darker legends to life with his sensational music.

The story of Kitty Jay is said to come from the 1790s. She was an orphan girl from a poorhouse who came to work on a Dartmoor farm. Raped by the farmer's son, she became pregnant, and such was her desperation and shame that she took her own life. The three local parishes refused to bury her in consecrated ground, so Kitty was interred at a crossroads on a shared boundary. No one knows who leaves the flowers at Jay's Grave to this day.

Tom Stratton
Deputy Land Steward, Duchy of Cornwall

Tom reached down and patted his lively but obedient black Labrador, who had greeted me earlier with a furiously wagging tail. Tom smiled, "Bea travels with me most days. She is ever so good and of course loves being on the moors. The place is so rugged and ever changing. Based at Princetown I have the good fortune to drive to work with views over the Dart valley and no journey is ever the same, it's a real privilege."

Although he was born and brought up in the New Forest, Tom Stratton's grandparents lived in Devon so he knew and loved Dartmoor from a young age. After training at Bicton and Seale Hayne agricultural colleges and qualifying as a chartered surveyor, he was appointed to the post of Deputy Land Steward for Dartmoor in the spring of 2008, having previously spent seven years working in other areas of the Duchy.

A third of Dartmoor National Park is owned by the Duchy of Cornwall, and Dartmoor is the largest of its extensive land-holdings, which stretch across some 23 counties of England. The Duchy has owned most of its 67,500 acres of Dartmoor since its creation in 1337 by Edward lll for his son, the Black Prince, who became the first Duke of Cornwall. The name of the Estate is derived from the Earldom of Cornwall, and it exists to provide an income from its assets for The Prince of Wales, currently Prince Charles, who is also Duke of Cornwall. Tom continued, "With such a history you might think we have not kept pace with the modern world, but the Duchy is very progressive. HRH has an insatiable appetite for new ideas and is very involved with estate management. He is particularly interested in farming, affordable housing, renewable energy and employment opportunities for young people."

In the past, mineral extraction and peat were important industries; today, agriculture dominates the land use. The Duchy owns 21 farms on Dartmoor whose tenants breed and rear hill cattle and sheep; some also keep ponies. While other students were having fun on a gap year after university, Prince Charles spent time working on a Dartmoor farm to get first-hand experience of the harsh conditions faced by his tenant farmers. "I know personally how tough the weather can get on the moor," said Tom seriously, after recently spending his first Christmas on his parents-in-law farm near Widecombe-in-the-Moor. "It was one of the worst winters I can remember, with deep snow. Keeping the water troughs filled with fresh water was really difficult. By the time I had re-filled all the troughs, the first had frozen solid again."

His Duchy work is very diverse and often unpredictable, as he explained: "Agriculture is our core business on both enclosed and common land, and there is a portfolio of residential and commercial properties. We have significant interests in Postbridge and Princetown, let alone military training and owning approximately 26 miles of river. No two days or two hours are the same," he laughed. "With reviews of estate management, rent reviews, re-letting and liaising with farmers over maintenance, I meet a wide range of interesting people and organisations every week."

Tom looked pensive for a moment. "The most rewarding part of my work is helping to provide opportunities for people, particularly through the provision of housing. I sit on many committees involved with the management of Dartmoor, to ensure that the Duchy can have a positive impact by providing a global picture of what is going on across the moor. For instance, we have recently helped to set up a wood-fuel co-operative, which is now providing locally produced timber to a number of biomass boilers within the Dartmoor area. The Duchy endeavours to lead by example, working closely with local people and organisations."

Away from the office Tom is very much involved with life on the moor. Married at Widecombe-in-the-Moor Church, he and his wife rode more than a mile from the ceremony on a pair of horses to their reception at the nearby family farm. His new bride elegantly rode side-saddle through the ancient village, no doubt to the delight of both locals and visitors that day.

Snow on the moors makes life tough for travellers but fun when roads are cleared.

Tony Halse
Head of Conservation Works, Dartmoor National Park Authority

Dartmoor seemed very distant from East Devon where Tony Halse was born and brought up. But his father was passionate about the hills dominating the western skyline and the family took every opportunity to spend time on the moors. Tony was trained as a draughtsman with Devon County Council and took up his first post with the National Park Authority as a cartographer, in 1978. "Mainly drawing up plans for car parks, maps and other projects involving landscaping rather than buildings," he explained.

Today, he is based at the works depot in the old railway sheds in Bovey Tracey. Many of the projects Tony oversees are hidden from view. "Shame really," he said with a wry smile. "Much of what we do is buried or flooded. Power and telephone lines removed from view, leat renovation and restoring and stabilising washed-out river banks using large granite boulders. Most people don't even notice the work we've done, but then I suppose that's the way it should be.

Other projects are more visible, like information boards or toilet signs carved in stone. We even re-cut the letters of the Ten Commandments at Buckland Beacon. And do you know," he added, trying to look indignant, "people walk all over some of our handiwork!" He then explained: "We restored Cobble Lane in Lustleigh and the cobbles outside Dunsford Post Office.

"Some jobs are very satisfying though, like rescuing the Thornworthy Cist." Tony went on to describe how the ancient tomb was retrieved from Torquay museum and put back together again, sides and capping stone in the garden of the High Moorland Visitor Centre. "We were watched by TV cameras, so no pressure there," he laughed. "And jobs like that all need highly skilled masonry work," he pointed out.

Stone crosses are located all over the moor, with many in need of repair from time to time. "A recent, exciting find by local walkers", said Tony, leading me out into the works yard, "is this one." He gently stroked a raised carving of a cross on a large piece of granite. "Some ramblers noticed it upside-down in a wall on the King Way, and this is only half of it.

Sadly the other bit is missing, so we will make up a base plinth before re-erecting it on the same spot."

Wherever Tony travels these days he says he finds it hard to look at the view. His expert eye is constantly scanning walls, stone paths and memorials. "I suppose it's an occupational hazard," he laughed. But of all the varied work he has been so proudly involved with, the archaeological ones seem most special. "Dartmoor granite is amazing," he said, fondly patting another piece of rock. "Not just for its looks but for what you can do with it. And I have been very fortunate to work with some hugely talented craftsmen and contractors over the years. Heavy stuff though. I wish I could always call on the transport we used to take a supply of walling stone out to a remote location, in order to protect a newly exposed cist." I looked at him quizzically. "By helicopter," he said casually.

Tony's favourite works on the moor are the stone path to Grimspound and the restoration of some clapper bridges. "We needed a helping hand with those huge stones in the form of very big machines. How they did it years ago with just people, you have to admire," he added. But then Tony appreciates the planning, skill and back-breaking work required to improve and maintain the experience of visitors and local residents in the National Park more than most of us.

A local landmark, the 'Ten Commandments' was originally engraved in 1928. It was re-cut in 2007.

129

Jane Marchand

Senior Archaeologist, Dartmoor National Park Authority

The Dartmoor landscape is not so different from Jane Marchand's native north Wales, so she has always felt very much at home in Devon. Digging for a living does not sound like one of the most glamorous jobs in the world but that is what archaeologists adore. Holding a piece of flint and recognising the telltale marks of its making, with the knowledge that you are the first human to hold it for several thousand years, obviously gives Jane a real 'buzz'. "Dartmoor is such an exhilarating and fulfilling place to be an archaeologist. I feel so privileged to work in an area I love, a job which can be so enjoyable and the purpose of which is ever more widely appreciated."

Much of Jane's work is away from the cutting edge of trowel and shovel. It involves caring for and preserving the often-fragile remnants of past human activity for future generations. Planning walks and talks, interpreting ancient finds, and working with others to help preserve the past may seem a far cry from scraping at a hole in the ground, but it is just as

vital. You do not have to be an archaeologist to appreciate the extraordinary wealth of both Bronze Age and earlier remains found across the moor, although it naturally helps.

Jane's particular passion is for flint tools - fine arrowheads, scrapers and knives. Even the tiniest flake can tell an incredible story. Flint is not found naturally on Dartmoor, so any pieces discovered here must have been brought to the location by people. Even the location itself tells us something about the folk that fashioned them, as Jane explained: "Sometimes we find evidence of a working area where the flint was knapped; lots of discarded bits lie all around. Perhaps the site was a temporary camp, but sometimes it is simply beside a stream or a high point where the Stone Age hunter had a good view." This also tells us that the inhabitants that lived here all those years ago were not much different from us in their appreciation of a vantage point: "It brings us into direct contact with those prehistoric people who sat on the same spot and enjoyed the same surroundings as we do today."

When Channel 4's *Time Team* visited Dartmoor in the summer of 2010, their discoveries exceeded all expectations.

Far left: A Bronze Age flint arrowhead from 2600–1600 BC, found near Gidleigh, east Dartmoor.

Left: A potsherd known as 'Trevisker Ware' from Bellever roundhouse, 1610–1210 BC.

Amid the media circus, a breathless television presenter racing around, mud-splattered experts and people poring over the latest ground radar results, there emerged a fascinating portrait of prehistoric life. Set in a natural amphitheatre on the edge of the moor, stone rows, a large stone circle and worked flint revealed a previously unknown ceremonial site used for millennia.

Today, scientific advances have revolutionised the investigation of ancient sites but, incredible as it may seem, Dartmoor is still relatively unexplored in terms of its archaeology. Only a few modern excavations have taken place; most happened many years ago when techniques of recording and interpretation were often crude by today's standards and digs could even prove damaging. In addition to *Time Team*'s work, new excavations of a Bronze Age roundhouse and a burial cist on the north moor revealed exciting new evidence. Empathy is important for an archaeologist; so too is experience.

Dartmoor is obviously a very special place for Jane: "The feeling of continuity and timelessness one experiences working in a landscape that has been largely shaped by humans over thousands of years; people who left such remarkable evidence of the way they lived, worked and buried their dead." Jane's talent for reading a tiny piece of flint opens a tantalising window on their long-lost world.

Philip Coaker

Farmer and Chairman of the Dartmoor Farmers Association

It takes a hardy breed of cattle, sheep or pony to thrive in the middle of the moor, and a special breed of farmer to rear them. Philip Coaker is the fifth generation to farm at Runnage on the high moor near Postbridge. His great-great-grandfather came here in 1843, so Philip has a real sense of history. "I'm not a pioneer now, just a caretaker," he explained, "and my son is following in the family tradition to be a Dartmoor farmer. We have 220 acres up here and almost as much again lower down around Ashburton and Buckfast, where we can overwinter our animals. It's tough this high during the coldest months but it's good land, almost stone free." He added with a smile, "Today we can plough six to seven inches without hitting anything, but that is what five generations of stone removal can do."

Philip is a stockman at heart, proud of the prize-winning animals he breeds, despite having some tough acts to follow. His great-grandfather was once presented with a trophy from King George V. His father won more, including several Challenge cups that he received so often he was eventually allowed to keep them. Philip and his mother Alice donated a new perpetual memorial trophy in memory of Philip's father, Richard. It is something Philip is very proud of when he is fortunate to win it, which he does quite regularly at the annual breeds show and sale. He admitted, "We always enjoy winning it back again."

Born to be a farmer, Philip started his training early. At the age of 13 he was given his first sheep to enable him to rear his own flock. It obviously takes talent, a good eye and hard work to breed the best animals. "We have three types of sheep," he said. "My finest are the pedigree Whiteface Dartmoor, which we regularly show. My father was a founder member of the Whiteface Dartmoor Sheep Breeders Association. We also have a commercial flock of Texel-Suffolk crosses as well as our hill stock, the Scottish Blackface, which graze the common lands along with our ponies."

The management of the moor falls mainly to its farmers, using controlled burning and grazing as their most important tools. Philip is Vice-chairman of the Forest of Dartmoor Commoners' Association, whose members graze some 28,000 acres of the moor. As he explained, "The original Forest of Dartmoor was once the historic hunting ground of kings and princes, then for many years almost anyone could graze their stock on the moor. In 1985 the Dartmoor Commoners' Council created a register of marks and brands of grazing animals, so they could all be identified. The Dartmoor Commons Act of that year was a groundbreaking achievement, giving the public a right of access some 20 years ahead of the creation of common lands nationally. It also cemented the relationship between the Dartmoor National Park Authority and Dartmoor farmers."

Philip needs no excuse to enthuse about his animals. "We also have a herd of South Devon cattle. Not the big South Hams variety, but three-quarters the size, a smaller, tougher and darker kind, ideally suited to the moors; calm, quiet creatures. The family has always bred them and we've only ever bought a few cattle in all the years we've been here," he exclaimed. "Although livestock shows are exciting and an opportunity to show off your finest, for me the best time is when checking my South Devons out grazing on the open moorland, especially early on a bright summer's morning when they are still lying down. It's a picture of contentment," he added. "If they're happy, then so am I."

Controlled burning, known as swaling, is a vital part of moorland management by Dartmoor farmers.

Norman Baldock
Senior Ecologist, Dartmoor National Park Authority

For any child, a close encounter with the wild is a sure way to stimulate an interest in nature. Norman was no exception. A native of Widecombe-in-the-Moor, where his father was the headmaster of the local school, he was immersed in Dartmoor life from birth. That included enjoying the famous Widecombe-in-the-Moor Fair, waiting for the snow plough to appear after a heavy fall of snow, and maintaining the inevitable childhood mini zoo of moorland caterpillars, bugs and beetles. Many of his school friends came from farming families and that background helps when it comes to advising landowners on wildlife conservation. After a spell spent working with Wildlife Trusts elsewhere in England it was no surprise he returned to Dartmoor at the earliest opportunity.

Much of Norman's early work in the National Park was a journey of discovery. Wildlife surveys confirmed the presence of many rare and unusual plants and animals. For a naturalist nothing is more exciting than finding a rare wild beast or, even better, a completely new species. Norman's first sighting of a rare damselfly, previously unknown on the moors and confined to a single ditch, was the beginning of an important conservation initiative to protect and enhance the area. The southern damselfly is a beautiful, delicate creature, rare in Britain and declining elsewhere across southern Europe. Success was slow to start with but the arrival of the cavalry, albeit in the form of a small herd of Dartmoor ponies, appeared just in time. Norman explained: "Their grazing has helped transform the management of the surrounding damp grasslands and wet areas to the benefit of the southern damselfly and all its kind. Once almost extinct, they are now increasing in numbers."

It is not every day you can help save a species, let alone come across something new to science. The rediscovery of a flower and the finding of a tiny moth have added a new dimension to the growing list of Dartmoor's special wildlife. "The great thing about my job is that you never know what will turn up next. I have my favourites that for me capture the essence of the moor. Ravens evoke the windy wildness and rugged nature of the upland landscape, and the beauty of bog asphodels flowering and marsh fritillary butterflies is simply a joy to see." However, not everyone is pleased to be surprised by wildlife. "Every year we get a visitor calling to tell us that someone has released snakes on the moor. When I explain they are native and venomous, it does not always go down too well!"

Norman confessed that occasionally he yearns to see a few other creatures. He is still waiting to spot one of the most dramatic birds of prey, a red kite, soaring over Dartmoor. "And who knows, perhaps one day red squirrels and pine martens might return," he said hopefully. Luck often plays a huge part in wildlife watching, and nature is often unpredictable.

The antics of ecologists can occasionally provide some free entertainment, as witnessed by one landowner. "While advising on a large, rough area full of head-high and very dense bracken, we discussed the management of a field in the area while standing on a Devon bank that formed the field's boundary. When I suggested that I would need to look at the ground below to see if it had any value for wildlife, I jumped into the field and nearly fainted with shock as a huge red deer stag, that had been hidden asleep, rose and stomped off, head held high and snorting in indignation. The landowner himself nearly fell off the hedge bank with laughter."

Bog asphodel and cross-leaved heath can be found flowering in July.

Simon Dell, MBE
Special Constable and Dartmoor guide

While his young brothers played on the East Okement River, as a child Simon Dell could only gaze in awe at the surroundings. He had fallen in love with Dartmoor. Still a schoolboy living in North Devon, he grew up with the stories of author Henry Williamson - one in particular caught his imagination, namely *Tarka the Otter*. Soon he was following in the tracks of Tarka by walking up to Cranmere Pool and back down the River Taw. That first big Dartmoor walk was to inspire the rest of his life.

As a teenager he completed the Ten Tors Challenge more times than was sensible. And as an experienced mountaineer he served as a member and Chairman of the Dartmoor Rescue Group for two decades. Yet he always wanted to be a policeman. So working on Dartmoor for most of his service with the Devon and Cornwall Constabulary combined the best of both worlds. He describes himself 'like a stick of rock, a policeman through and through', eventually becoming a Special Constabulary Inspector for West Devon. When he

was later injured in the line of duty he received the Queen's Commendation for Bravery and national newspaper awards. After 30 years' service he retired in September 2007 to become the Crimebeat Coordinator for the Constabulary, working with young people in partnership with the High Sheriffs of each county. This work now takes him into schools, colleges and youth clubs where he engages youngsters in crime prevention and safety initiatives. As a result he was also awarded the Anne Frank Educator's Award.

A policeman's lot on Dartmoor was often hard and hazardous, especially when chasing escaped prisoners from Princetown. Once he apprehended an escapee dressed in sports kit. Both he and his charge, drenched and shivering with cold, were sent to Tavistock Hospital. Here he was made to wait, soaked to the skin in uniform, while the prisoner was given a hot bath. Then, to add insult to injury, the nurse chastised him for getting the poor man in such a state!

In those distant days policing was done mainly on foot or by bike. "If a car was needed in a hurry," remembered Simon, "I had to flag down a member of the public. Once an elderly lady in a Morris Minor gave me a lift to a road accident but only drove at 15mph. Eventually, I asked her politely to pull over and swapped to another car. After arriving in Merrivale I checked the casualties were OK and started sorting out the traffic. It was a while before the lady in the Morris Minor reached me. She wound down her window and proudly announced that she had just dropped off another constable on the way," Simon laughed.

"On another occasion a new superior officer arrived at a checkpoint to help us search cars for a prisoner. He was slow compared to the constables; the traffic quickly built up and people became impatient. So when the officer spotted another car overtaking the line, he assumed it was an emergency and waved it through. Later they learnt, much to the constables' amusement, that the car the Inspector had happily let pass was driven by the prisoner."

Simon has led an eventful life serving moorland communities more than most, but still vividly recalls his first sight of heather, bogs and tors, and revels in the cry of curlew and the song of skylarks. He has trudged across the moor searching for lost souls or chasing prisoners more times than he cares to remember. Now he is enjoying his retirement from full-time policing, if that is what his still active life can be called, yet he remains in hope that he will catch a glimpse of Tarka in the head-waters of the Taw as he makes his way home.

The classic story of *Tarka the Otter* beautifully captured the life of a Dartmoor river and the imagination of a child.

Tony Beard
Farmer, broadcaster and entertainer

Known and loved as the 'The Wag from Widecombe', Tony Beard's popular BBC Radio Devon appearances provide a real taste of Dartmoor - good humour, wonderful stories and friendly chatter. You can even imagine a cream tea, with the jam always on top of the cream. Tony still lives in the farmhouse where he was born with views to Buckland Beacon.

It is difficult to imagine this engaging performer as a shy youngster, yet once he was. His parents led a quiet life running a small dairy herd, supplying milk to neighbours around Widecombe-in-the-Moor, which Tony delivered in enamel churns. "We didn't have a car," said Tony in his warm Devon voice, "and my mother was not well, so we didn't travel far." The farm was his playground and his lifelong interest in archaeology was sparked by a lucky find. "I was six when, trying to catch a mole to earn some pocket money, I found this flint arrowhead. "'Tis Bronze Age, over 3,500 years old," he said, still amazed by the discovery; he

then produced a wonderful collection of similar finds, some even older. Wildlife, too, became a childhood passion, one time feeding caterpillars in a jar to later release hundreds of peacock butterflies. It became clear that Tony has always had a thirst for knowledge. "I had only ever been to Plymouth once with my uncle to see a pantomime before I won a scholarship to Plymouth College," he mentioned casually. It was a prize his parents could never have afforded, until Tony passed his 11+ exam. "One of the top three scores in the country," he admitted modestly. "My uncle dropped me off on my first day at school and said he would pick me up in eight weeks' time. It was daunting but I made some great friends."

Tony discovered his talent for public speaking with the Newton Abbot Young Farmers Club and the opportunity this organisation gave him to hone his skills. "We used to write a topic on a piece of paper, put 'em all in a hat, then draw one out to speak for a minute. My first was 'necking in barley'. For us farmers necking can be a problem with the crop, but of course you can read anything you like into those words. I started by saying you 'ave to be careful what you say in a field of barley, there's lots of ears about." But, as Tony's many radio listeners know, he has a real way with words. A tireless campaigner for all things Dartmoor, he gained his 'Wag from Widecombe' label over 45 years ago on a billboard for a cabaret act in Ashburton. Now well accustomed to audiences from one man and a dog to over three thousand, Tony was born to be a broadcaster. "My BBC appearances started with an invitation to do just six Sunday programmes. Then 15 years on they realised I still 'adn't signed a contract," he chuckled.

Farming is still in Tony's blood although he sold his herd of cattle not long after the foot-and-mouth crisis in 2001. Today, his involvement in Dartmoor history and the famous Widecombe Fair, a past President of the Devonshire Association, let alone radio and stage appearances, keep him busy as the moor's best-known ambassador, all-round entertainer and treasure trove of local knowledge. "Funny things 'appen to me," he laughed. "Back in 1959 I remembered seeing a carved working model of 'Uncle Tom Cobley and All', but no one else did. Then, after the 'istory of the Fair was published, I 'ad a phone call. Someone 'ad found the model stored in bits in three boxes in Launceston," he exclaimed, looking surprised. "Now, with the 'elp of members of our local 'istory group, it's on display in the church." Today, Uncle Tom Cobley would be proud of the part he plays in keeping Dartmoor traditions alive and would feel he has a great successor in Tony Beard.

Buckland Beacon is a popular, easily reached viewpoint offering magnificent all-round vistas.

Why Dartmoor is special

The blanket bogs of the high moor form the principal river catchment for most of Devon and East Cornwall.

The ever-changing weather and harshness of the climate shaped the culture of its people and their buildings. Communities adapted to their challenging surroundings with a distinctive dialect and deep-rooted traditions.

Dartmoor has a climate of extremes – sometimes hot and tinder dry, more often cold and wet. Lashed by howling winds and driving rain, shrouded in mist or lost in low cloud, Dartmoor is a tough place for life to thrive year-round.

The distinctive granite tors are surrounded by rock-strewn slopes.

The ancient upwelling of molten granite subjected the surrounding sedimentary rocks to immense heat and pressure. This process formed many minerals around the edge of its molten mass, including lead, copper and silver.

The largest unbroken moorland in the south of England offers visitors an unrivalled opportunity to roam freely in almost any direction they choose.

Ancient oak woodland of international importance, as well as large areas of heath and bog, have combined to create a wildlife community like no other on Earth.

The use of moorland common for grazing cattle, sheep and ponies has remained the same for thousands of years. Two distinct breeds of sheep and the native Dartmoor pony are all officially recognised.

A remarkable richness of human activity stretches back over 8,000 years, from early farming to tin mining, and a pattern of medieval settlements survive to the present day.

The highest upland in southern England dominates Devon with its wide horizons and impressive views. Yet during the Ice Ages, Dartmoor remained free of glaciers.

Dartmoor is one of the few places in England where peace and quiet allow the sounds of the natural world to reign supreme. Here one experiences a real sense of wilderness and, with true dark after sunset, an opportunity to truly appreciate the vastness of the night sky.

It is a landscape of myth and legend, where art and literature is inspired. Here a wonderful timelessness pervades, the modern world seems hours away, and village life still flourishes. On the moor anyone can escape to refresh his or her very soul.

Index